Get That Hope

Get That Hope

Andrea Scott

Get That Hope
first published 2024 by Scirocco Drama
An imprint of J. Gordon Shillingford Publishing Inc.
© 2024 Andrea Scott

Scirocco Drama Editor: Glenda MacFarlane
Cover design by Doowah Design
Author photo by Tanja Tiziana
Production photos by David Hou

Printed and bound in Canada on 100% post-consumer recycled paper.

Performance inquiries to:
Colin Rivers, Marquis Entertainment
colin@mqent.ca

Library and Archives Canada Cataloguing in Publication

Title: Get that hope / Andrea Scott.
Names: Scott, Andrea, 1971- (Playwright), author.
Identifiers: Canadiana 20240455193 | ISBN 9781990738616 (softcover)
Subjects: LCGFT: Drama.
Classification: LCC PS8637.C675 G48 2024 | DDC C812/.6—dc23

We acknowledge the financial support of the Canada Council for the Arts, the Government of Canada, the Manitoba Arts Council, and the Manitoba Government for our publishing program.

J. Gordon Shillingford Publishing
P.O. Box 86, RPO Corydon Avenue, Winnipeg, MB Canada R3M 3S3

This play is dedicated to Wesley Scott.

Andrea Scott

Andrea Scott's play *Eating Pomegranates Naked* won the RBC Arts Professional Award, and was named Outstanding Production at the 2013 SummerWorks Festival. *Better Angels: A Parable* won the SummerWorks Award for Outstanding Production in 2015. Both plays were published in 2018 (Scirocco Drama). *Don't Talk to Me Like I'm Your Wife* won the Cayle Chernin Award for Theatre and was produced at SummerWorks in 2016. In 2019, *Every Day She Rose*, co-written with Nick Green, wowed audiences at Buddies in Bad Times and was published by Playwrights Canada Press. Scott's play about civil rights pioneer Viola Desmond, *Controlled Damage*, had its sold-out world premiere at Neptune Theatre in 2020, and was published by Scirocco Drama later that year. *Get That Hope* had its world premiere at the Stratford Festival in 2024.

Andrea also writes for television. She currently divides her time between Toronto and Hollywood, California.

Acknowledgements

Akiva Romer-Segal

Antoni Cimolino

André Sills

b current Performing Arts Co.

Canada Council

Colin Rivers

Dave Auster

Fay Scott

Joanna Falck

Keith Barker

Marquis Entertainment

Ontario Arts Council

Obsidian Theatre

Soulpepper Theatre

Stratford Festival

Studio 180

Tarragon Theatre

Toronto Arts Council

Wesley Scott

Esther Jun

Playwright's Note: All in the Family

Do you think when Sartre penned the words, "Hell is other people," he was clutching a glass of Naked Grape Merlot, hunched in an upstairs closet, hiding from his family at Thanksgiving? What I've learned over the last few years is a lot of us have families that make us squirrelly. We love (some of) them but there are times when one just needs a break from their voices, clothes, walk, and, well, everything.

My parents are two Jamaicans who'd been raised by their grandparents, as is common in the West Indies. They did not know how to give me the family experiences we all watched on shows such as *My Three Sons*, *That's So Raven*, *Little House on the Prairie*, and *Family Matters*.

My father never knocked on my bedroom door to ask, upon opening, if I was okay. My mom didn't stoop down, look me in the eye and say, "You can always talk to me, hon." And my siblings weren't good-natured goofballs who called me "Champ." TV lied to me. TV lied to all of us. Real families are messy, irritating, sad, laden with trauma, and laced with some very happy memories. Have you seen Season 2, Episode 6 of *The Bear*? It's a far more honest representation of the contemporary family unit and it ends with a car crashing through the living room.

Over a year ago, I was invited to have dinner with my friend's family. I'd never met them before and was very excited to meet the people my friend talked about all the time. It was great. I met the parents, older brother, adorable nephew, quiet sister-in-law, and was treated to an incredible meal. This was a fun, tight, funny family, but my friend's demeanour changed gradually when we were with them. They ribbed him, interrupted when he tried to explain things to me, and generally caused him to get very frustrated. After being corrected on one more thing, he abruptly he left the table and didn't return for almost fifteen minutes.

I sat there making awkward small talk. Thank goodness his parents are funny. Eventually he returned, sat beside me, and resumed eating. When I whispered, "Is everything okay?" all I got in return was a curt nod. The next day I received a text from him. "Now that you've met my family, do I make sense?" And you know what, dear readers? He did.

As I write this in June 2024, I'm in the middle of another family dynamic: the workplace. I'm a writer on a TV show in Los Angeles and have been since January. There are ten of us. We spend Monday to Friday together from ten to six (sometimes later). When we break for lunch, we eat together and then go for a walk. We're on a group chat thread where jokes, memes, and confessions fly back and forth for, sometimes, hours. This was all well and good until I just got sick of everyone. Actually, I think the feeling was mutual on some days. The sound of another's voice and their frequent pauses as they pitched an idea made me nuts. And if I didn't have misophonia before I left Canada, I do now.

But here's the thing about family: you love them to the ends of the earth and there's nobody you want to share news with more than your family, chosen, or otherwise. I don't want to see anyone in my close circle upset, disappointed or hurt. And the feeling is mutual, even if it's awkwardly expressed sometimes. That's what I tried to convey in *Get That Hope*. When you watch the play, you may see your auntie, brother, dad, sister, or even yourself. Will you be kind and forgiving? I hope you walk out of the theatre with a level of understanding and calm in your heart that at the end of that frazzled day, you are loved, and everything's going to be alright.

Peace and Hair Grease, Andrea Scott

P.S. Directors: this play runs at a clip. Ready? Set. GO!

Foreword

By Marcia Johnson

I am familiar with many a kitchen sink drama. *Get That Hope* stands out for me as the first one set in the kitchen of a Jamaican-Canadian family in Toronto; the kind of kitchen that I grew up in. As I write this, the Stratford 2024 premiere production of *Get That Hope* is still months away, but I have had the pleasure of reading the script. While doing so, I understood what it must feel like to be a Newfoundlander watching David French's plays or a Québécois seeing the plays of Michel Tremblay.

Playwrights of Jamaican heritage are not rare in Canada, especially in Toronto, but, as far as I'm aware, Andrea Scott is the first to apply this cultural background to the familiar kitchen sink treatment. I'm proud (and a little bit jealous) of my friend for beating me to it.

What really thrills me about Andrea getting the Stratford commission is that this prominent theatre is showing that, like with French, Tremblay and many others, family stories are universal. Andrea doesn't sugar-coat or idealize the family that she has created. Audiences will see that this Jamaican family has members, as with other family dramas, who are imperfect and maybe even unlikeable at times.

From the very beginning of the play, with the playing of the Jamaican national anthem, Andrea stakes her claim. One of the props in the description of the archetypal home is a framed and lit photograph of Pierre Trudeau, the prime minister who famously created the multiculturalism policy. It was made official in 1971, but Jamaicans and people from other Caribbean islands were part of a huge immigration wave in the mid- to late 1960s. As these islands were members of the Commonwealth, citizens could travel to Canada without a visa. They could also take advantage of several programs including the very popular domestic workers cohort. Even earlier, in 1962 (the year of Jamaica's independence, celebrated in *Get That Hope*), skin colour was no longer a deterrent to acceptance in the country. (Yes, skin colour used to be a factor in immigration, but that's another story.) Emphasis was now placed "…on their education and skills." *(The Canadian Encyclopedia)* As a side note, I am impressed that Andrea has included the character Millicent, a character from the Philippines, as Margaret's personal support worker. This is a demonstration of how simple it is to be inclusive. Millicent is not, moreover, a token. Her role is integral.

The Whytes will take their place in Canadian theatre history alongside French's Mercers. They will speak in their own dialect the way that Tremblay's characters spoke *joual*. Anglophones missed out on that nuance, but the excellent translations drew us into the working-class stories.

In *Get That Hope*, there are elements early in the very first scene that place the Whytes firmly and unapologetically in Jamaican culture. The mention of Milo drink mix, ackee and saltfish and yardies will elicit nods of recognition, laughter and even a few utterances from certain audience members. People who were encouraged to come to Canada from that small island decades ago, who looked after Canadian-born children and worked in factories before settling here and raising their own children, are now having their stories told, are now being acknowledged at the Stratford Shakespeare Festival. This is a big deal and it is long overdue. Notably, *Get That Hope* is a stand-alone show; not an adaptation, or the "Black version" of an existing play from the European canon. What a vote of confidence from Stratford.

The Festival is saying that a play from this specific Black culture is enough. It does not need to reference or pay homage to anyone or anything.

What a moment we are having. And by "we" I don't mean just Jamaican-Canadians. I mean "we" as theatregoers. This signals a broadening of our horizons. I applaud Stratford for taking this deliberate step.

I also applaud Scirocco Drama for publishing a play that contains dialogue written in patois. This kind of acknowledgement is so important. Theatre artists of colour in Canada have struggled to be included over the years. Tired of waiting and tired of playing stereotypical roles, a brave selection of these artists created Black Theatre Workshop, Obsidian Theatre Company, fu-Gen, Cahoots etc. Not only did they produce successful plays, they also set up mentorship programs and playwrights' units. (I was a member of Obsidian's first playwrights' unit.) People from underrepresented groups started coming to theatre for the first time to see their stories on stage. Regular theatregoers came out, too.

I am so happy for artists who are entering this more inclusive theatre landscape. There have been many times during my career where I thought that we had turned a corner and there would be more work available for me and other artists of colour. Then things would go back to "normal." I don't think that there's any going back this time. *Get That Hope* is history-making, and I can't wait to see it in the flesh.

—Marcia Johnson, Spring 2024

Marcia Johnson is a playwright and actor based in Toronto. Her plays include *Serving Elizabeth*, *Courting Johanna*, *Late* and *Say Ginger Ale*

Production History

Production Stage Manager:.................... Michael Hart

Production Assistant:...............Kate Munro-Bergfeldt

One more thing…I wish I could say *Get That Hope* sprung fully formed out of my head, effortlessly and without pain. Alas, I had an incredible midwife in Keith Barker, Stratford's Director of New Plays. He asked the right questions, shared his own personal stories about filial obligation, and pushed me when I wanted to take the easy way out. His enthusiasm for the play was contagious and it buoyed me when I had doubts. I couldn't have created the play without him. Miigwetch.

Conrad Coates as Richard Whyte in *Get That Hope*. Stratford Festival 2024. Playwright: Andrea Scott. Director: André Sills. Set and costume designer: Sarah Uwadiae. Lighting Designer: Steve Lucas. Photo by David Hou.

Savion Roach as Simeon Whyte with Celia Aloma as Rachel Whyte in *Get That Hope*. Stratford Festival 2024. Playwright: Andrea Scott. Director: André Sills. Set and costume designer: Sarah Uwadiae. Lighting Designer: Steve Lucas. Photo by David Hou.

Kim Roberts as Margaret Whyte and Conrad Coates as Richard
Whyte with Jennifer Villaverde as Millicent Flores (left) in *Get That
Hope*. Stratford Festival 2024. Playwright: Andrea Scott. Director:
André Sills. Set and costume designer: Sarah Uwadiae. Lighting
Designer: Steve Lucas. Photo by David Hou.

Savion Roach as Simeon Whyte in *Get That Hope*. Stratford Festival
2024. Playwright: Andrea Scott. Director: André Sills. Set and
costume designer: Sarah Uwadiae. Lighting Designer: Steve Lucas.
Photo by David Hou.

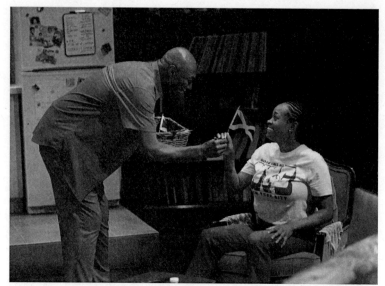

Conrad Coates as Richard Whyte and Celia Aloma as Rachel Whyte in *Get That Hope*. Stratford Festival 2024. Playwright: Andrea Scott. Director: André Sills. Set and costume designer: Sarah Uwadiae. Lighting Designer: Steve Lucas. Photo by David Hou.

Celia Aloma as Rachel Whyte in *Get That Hope*. Stratford Festival 2024. Playwright: Andrea Scott. Director: André Sills. Set and costume designer: Sarah Uwadiae. Lighting Designer: Steve Lucas. Photo by David Hou.

Jennifer Villaverde as Millicent Flores and Celia Aloma as Rachel Whyte in *Get That Hope*. Stratford Festival 2024. Playwright: Andrea Scott. Director: André Sills. Set and costume designer: Sarah Uwadiae. Lighting Designer: Steve Lucas. Photo by David Hou.

From Left: Jennifer Villaverde as Millicent Flores, Savion Roach as Simeon Whyte, Conrad Coates as Richard Whyte, Celia Aloma as Rachel Whyte, and Kim Roberts as Margaret Whyte in *Get That Hope*. Stratford Festival 2024. Playwright: Andrea Scott. Director: André Sills. Set and costume designer: Sarah Uwadiae. Lighting Designer: Steve Lucas. Photo by David Hou.

Characters

Rachel Whyte:
32, Black, striver, anxious but outwardly self-assured.

Rachel is a high-achieving Black woman who never thinks she's doing enough. Her dark skin makes her feel like an outsider in the family. There are not enough hours in the day to get everything done and yet, where does the emptiness come from? She is taking another class to improve herself in a demanding job market. She still lives at home with her parents to help them out with the rent since her stepmother's been off work on disability.

Sergeant Simeon Whyte:
28, Black, Rachel's brother, veteran, suffering from PTSD.

Simeon is the youngest, the baby, and in Rachel's eyes, the favourite. He's Margaret and Richard's first-born and bears a resemblance to his mother, who is light-skinned. A soldier with PTSD after an incident he cannot discuss without being re-traumatized, he joined the military to prove he had a purpose, but after the horrors he's witnessed, he is unmoored. Simeon also has a crippling fear of bridges that has negatively affected his life now that he's back in Canada as a civilian. Getting a job as a veteran has been difficult and has placed a strain on his relationships at home where he still lives with his sister and parents.

Margaret Whyte:
57, Black, the Matriarch, noble, quietly resentful.

Menopause has settled on her like a bitch and it's made her more insufferable than usual. Margaret feels everything. Attuned to everything her family is feeling causes her pain and makes her high-strung. Employed at a job that is meaningless to her, but stranded at home on disability after a fall, she's had more of an opportunity to see her family with all their corrosive flaws, and how she may have contributed to them.

Richard Whyte:
62, Black, the Patriarch, strong accent, charming, dreamer, secretive.

A dreamer who refuses to see the harshness of life in front of him and in his house. The reality of his wife's physical and emotional pain eludes him as he continues to believe in the far-off possibility that he'll win the lottery. He is unaware that the way he treats his oldest is deepening her resentment against him, even as she works three jobs to help the family stay afloat. He's an old school West Indian who believes the father should always be the king of the home, even if he can't always pay the bills.

Millicent Flores:
48, Filipina, PSW, the neighbour, selfless, heartbroken.

The long-time neighbour from upstairs who has adopted the Whyte family as her own. Too old to be treated like a daughter and too young to be seen as an auntie, she occupies a nebulous place in their home, for which she has a key. Popping in to check in on Margaret from time to time, and carrying on a secret affair with Simeon, Millicent has invoked Rachel's ire, causing her to wonder what her place is in a world that doesn't always see or respect her.

Sometimes you need a likkle bit o' suffering to get that hope!

Act One

Scene 1

RECORDING: Please stand for the national anthem.

Hopefully, the audience will stand and listen, respectfully.

The Jamaican national anthem, "Jamaica, Land We Love," is played loudly for fifteen seconds.

Offstage we hear yelling:

MARGARET: *(O/S.)* Stop ya noise! Ye hear me? Just stop. Stop stop stop stop…

This should go on until MARGARET enters; she's yelling at her husband, RICHARD, who is singing the last few bars. He need not be any good.

Ah, why you even know that anymore, eh? If you gonna sing, I want to hear "O Canada" or "Sweet Caroline," you hear?

RICHARD: You're a bad Jamaican, Meggy. You nuh even know the words anymore.

We are in the home of a Jamaican family. The room is jumbled but loved, with framed, lit portraits of Pierre Trudeau and

Barack Obama displayed prominently on the back wall. A medium-sized djembe sits on the ground between the photos of the kids, family and Justin Trudeau. The sofa is covered in plastic; there are doilies on every surface, and a sparkly map of Jamaica on the wall. The beeps, crashes, and bangs from construction happening outside occasionally bleed in.

It's August 6. Present Day.

RICHARD runs to fat but is still handsome and smooth on his feet as he guides his wife, MARGARET, light-skinned and a beauty, across the living room in dance. They are still very much in love and enjoy being together, in spite of their periodic bickering.

MARGARET picks up the newspaper and flips through it absently. The sun shines through the window and catches the shine in her hair and highlights her wrinkle-free, golden-brown skin. She looks a decade younger than her age, but the beads of sweat belie the menopause. RICHARD sits beside his wife in an armchair, staring at her with a smile.

MARGARET: Is your daughter still asleep?

RICHARD: Gimme dat.

MARGARET hands him the section of the paper she's holding. RICHARD flips through it. MARGARET looks offstage, while fanning herself with the sports section.

MARGARET: I want some tea.

RICHARD: I get a good feeling today, Meggy.

MARGARET:	She should be up by now.
RICHARD:	Let her sleep.
MARGARET:	It's almost nine!
RICHARD:	You see the jackpot? And someone win, you know, right here in Toronto.
	MARGARET stands and looks down the hallway.
MARGARET:	*(Muttering.)* Thirty-odd-year-old woman still asleep at this time. What is this foolishness? Rachel!
RICHARD:	Hush, man.
MARGARET:	Rachel! Rachel Whyte! Get up!
RICHARD:	Come. Sit, girl. I'll make you some Milo as soon as I finish checking these numbers. This could be our last day as poor people.
MARGARET:	Me nuh want Milo. I want tea.
RICHARD:	On this day, of all of the days, you want to drink the colonizer's poison? Milo is our drink.
MARGARET:	And we not poor.
RICHARD:	We're not? Seventeen million. Lawd God! I'll take half that! Once we win, we can finally go back home to visit. And stay in a hotel, no staying with our families.
MARGARET:	What's wrong with *my* family?
RICHARD:	They're stoosh, but still have dem hand out when we land. *(Stands, stretches and walks over to the window.)*

MARGARET: We haven't been back home in over fifteen years. How you know they gonna have a handout?

RICHARD: Because that's how Jamaicans stay. And me talking 'bout your people *and* mine. The Reids and the Whytes; think we rich cuz we live in Canada.

MARGARET: Did you remember to fill my prescription?

RICHARD: I give it to Rachel to pick up.

MARGARET: Then she needs to get up.

RICHARD: She worked an overnight and didn't get in until three. *(Peeks out the window.)* Looks like it's gonna be a hot one today. Do I need to turn on the AC?

MARGARET: Yes. *(She fans harder.)*

>   *From the hallway we hear loud knocking and SIMEON's voice.*

SIMEON: *(O/S.)* Rachel! Did you fall in? I need to use the bathroom.

MARGARET: Well, at least Simeon is awake. Should get him to turn on the air. *(Bellows.)* Simeon! Simeon!

RICHARD: My wife, the trumpet. *(Chuckles.)*

MARGARET: *(Irritated.)* You know I don't like it when you call me that.

RICHARD: You know, we should've had ackee and saltfish for breakfast this morning. How you celebrate Independence Day without our national dish, eh?

MARGARET: I asked you to buy the ackee two weeks ago. You nuh remember dat?

RICHARD: And everywhere I go I see twelve ninety-nine a tin. A tin! For ackee…this city is full of crooks, you know? They know it's our day and you see how dem stay?

MARGARET: Richard! Nobody knows that but other yardies like you.

SIMEON enters. He's tall, the colour of caramel, and dressed in his Armed Forces uniform, but the shirt is still untucked.

RICHARD: *(Upon seeing his son.)* Soldier Boy!

SIMEON: Knows what? *(He kisses his mother on the cheek.)*

MARGARET: Mek me a cuppa tea, baby? *(She cranes her neck to look at him.)*

RICHARD: That it's Jamaica's Independence Day, when we finally get rid of the British!

MARGARET: *(Pleading.)* Tea?

SIMEON: Nobody knows that, Daddy. It's hot in here, Mummy, are you sure you want a tea?

MARGARET: Yes. Ah why you dress like dat?

SIMEON: Earl Grey or mint?

MARGARET: Surprise me.

RACHEL enters pulling off a sleep mask as SIMEON walks to the kitchen; she's looking at her phone. She keeps her hair natural; she radiates strength and intelligence, but she is tired, so tired. She pockets her phone and kisses her dad.

RACHEL: *(Sweetly.)* Happy Decolonization day, Daddy. *(Flat.)* Morning, Margaret.

MARGARET: *(To RACHEL.)* You nuh hear me call you a few minutes ago?

RICHARD: What you say, Rachel?

RACHEL: Today is the day our people raised our flag and kicked the Union Jack to the curb.

RICHARD: Ah! *(Laughs.)* You see that.

> *Belting with a strong voice, RACHEL sings a few bars of "Jamaica, Land We Love," until RICHARD joins in, while MARGARET grimaces.*

RICHARD: *(Pointing to RACHEL.)* That's my daughter.

MARGARET: That she is.

RICHARD: Good girl! And wha' Jamaica call before it name what it name?

RACHEL: Santiago.

RICHARD: Yes! I mek you some cornmeal porridge for breakfast. It pon de stove.

RACHEL: Thank you, Daddy.

MARGARET: How you remember that?

> *RACHEL shrugs.*

You a Canadian now.

RACHEL: So are you.

MARGARET: I hear it every day until I move to this country. Of course *I* remember.

RACHEL: I used to sing it when I walked to school every day. I just have a good memory.

RICHARD: *(Preening.)* She gets that from me.

SIMEON enters with a cup of tea and toasted hardo bread which he hands to his mother.

SIMEON: Talking about Rachet's memory?

RACHEL: Don't call me—

SIMEON: You still sensitive about that?

RICHARD: *(Muttering.)* Chuh! Colonizer's poison. I could drink some Milo right now… *(He begins to exit.)*

SIMEON: We're out. Sorry, Daddy.

MARGARET: *(Taking a bite of her toast.)* Did you get my prescription, Rachel? Your father said you picked it up yesterday. I need it.

RACHEL: Oh, yeah, it's in my room.

RACHEL exits.

RICHARD: And don't forget my lottery tickets. I need to check my numbers.

RACHEL: *(O/S.)* Okay, Daddy.

MARGARET: You must be so hot.

SIMEON: I'm gonna turn on the air. It's brutal in here.

SIMEON exits.

RICHARD: You look sharp, boy.

SIMEON: *(O/S.)* I'm… I have to go to a funeral.

RICHARD: *(To SIMEON.)* That reminds me, you remember Nancy?

SIMEON: *(O/S.)* Who?

MARGARET: He was eight when we live there, of course he doesn't remember.

RICHARD: Okay. Well, anyway, her mother-in-law die.

              SIMEON enters. RACHEL returns and hands the prescription to MARGARET.

SIMEON: *(Blankly.)* Oh yeah?

RACHEL: Aww, that's sad.

RICHARD: Yeah. Cancer. A bad one.

SIMEON: Is there such a thing as a good cancer?

RACHEL: Thyroid, skin, *(Plunks down on the sofa.)* prostate.

RICHARD: Did you know it was a Jamaican that cured prostate cancer?

MARGARET: Of course, the first cancer cured would be for a man and his ding-a-ling.

RACHEL: *(To MARGARET.)* Ding-a-ling?

              MARGARET screws up her face with distaste.

              There's no cure for prostate cancer, Daddy.

RICHARD: *(Stubborn.)* Yes, his name is Dr. Henry Lowe and he found the cure in ganja.

RACHEL: Did you get this information from the internet?

RICHARD: You know why we don't see this in the newspaper? Because prostate cancer kill more Black men than any of the other cancers AND it was a Black man. Did you remember my tickets, Rachel?

RACHEL: I forgot. Sorry. *(She rises to go to her room.)*

RICHARD: You always had such a good memory, wha'ppen?

RACHEL: I haven't had my coffee yet.

SIMEON: That reminds me, we're out of cream.

RACHEL: Simeon, if you're the last to finish something you have to replace it.

SIMEON: I said I was sorry. I'll pick some up on my way back.

RICHARD: Back from where?

MARGARET: A funeral. So, who die?

SIMEON: Remember Nadine? I brought her over a few years ago?

MARGARET: Nadine died?!

RICHARD: Who?

MARGARET: That nice girl with the blue blue eyes, right? When she come over, she brought you your favourite dessert, Richard.

SIMEON: Yeah, that was her.

RICHARD: *(Thinks for a moment.)* Eccles cake gyal! Oh no!

MARGARET: I'm so sorry, Simeon. She was sweet.

SIMEON: Thanks.

MARGARET: Why you have to dress in your uniform, though? Why you can't wear one of your suits?

SIMEON: Because we served together. It's a sign of respect.

MARGARET: Well, okay, okay, I don't know these things. Wasn't she the same age as you?

            SIMEON nods soberly.

MARGARET: *Drops her voice to a whisper.)* Was it cancer?

            RACHEL enters and hands a stack of lottery tickets to RICHARD.

RACHEL: That's not a polite question.

MARGARET: What? I'm curious. Is it wrong to be curious?

RICHARD: *(Quietly.)* Let me die in my sleep. No pain, no nothing.

SIMEON: She killed herself.

MARGARET: Oh my Lord…she commit suicide.

RACHEL: We say "died by suicide" now.

MARGARET: Who's "we"? And why you always have to be so smart, eh?

            RACHEL takes a deep breath, takes a piece of gum out of her purse, puts it in her mouth and chews.

RICHARD: What does it matter now? Still dead. Dead as a doornail. *(Chuckles.)* It's sad, though. You ever notice there are never any Black people in the obituaries in the paper? Never. *(Picks up the paper and turns to the obits.)*

MARGARET: And yet, we die all the same.

RICHARD: *(Flipping the pages.)* One, Two, Three, Four, Five. Six. Six pages of dead white people and not one Black face. Mm, mm, mm…no suh.

RACHEL: You're morbid.

RICHARD: You wait. You hit fifty and all you think about is death, death, death. You're going to die one day, too, you know.

RACHEL: Okay.

RICHARD: Won't be thirty forever.

RACHEL: *(Petulant.)* I'm thirty-two.

MARGARET: *(To SIMEON.)* You should put something in your belly, honey. Did you eat anything this morning?

SIMEON: I don't have an appetite. Actually, I should get going. I'm...one of the pallbearers. *(He starts to exit.)*

RACHEL: Are you okay?

SIMEON: I'm fine.

MARGARET: *(Quietly.)* I just don't understand why anyone would kill themselves. I just don't.

RICHARD: Life is wonderful. I love living. I'm never going to die.

MARGARET: You know, back home nobody would do that. Nobody. It just doesn't happen.

RICHARD: Of course it does. We just never hear about it. I mean, you mek it *back* from war and kill yourself? You *must* be mad. Yuh head no good!

MARGARET: Nah, man. You never see me do sumthing like dat.

RICHARD: 'Membah Bippy?

MARGARET: Bippy Holmes from Trelawny Parish? Wit the club foot and likkle arm?

RICHARD: *(Nods.)* Kill himself.

MARGARET: *(Shocked.)* No!

RICHARD: Cuckoo. 'Im jump from Dunn's River Falls. *(Mocking.)* I can fly!! *(Chuckles.)* Crazy, crazy, man…

SIMEON: Don't call people crazy.

RICHARD: But if you crazy, you crazy, nuh?!

MARGARET: Everybody is so sensitive now. Can't say commit suicide, can't say crazy, what's next? Can't say Black? Can't say chupid or eediot? *(Kisses her teeth.)* You Canadian kids are so soft.

RACHEL: It's called having compassion.

SIMEON: Rach, it's okay. / I'm fine.

MARGARET: It's war! What you expect? You go foreign to kill people, you're not going to be happy, right?

SIMEON: We were peacekeepers!

RICHARD: How you keep peace / in a warzone? Nevah understand that.

RACHEL: You're not fine. / You don't have to be fine.

SIMEON: *(Firm.)* I'm fine—

              SIMEON exits.

RACHEL: I need to get out of here—

SIMEON: What?

RACHEL: Thank you for the porridge, Daddy!

              RACHEL exits.

RICHARD:	I mek sure to use lots of condensed milk and nutmeg.
SIMEON:	*(Turns to MARGARET.)* Have you taken your pills?
MARGARET:	You're so sweet. Such a good boy. No, I haven't taken any since I just got them from Rachel. Can I get another cup of tea?
SIMEON:	You haven't finished the first one.
MARGARET:	*(Whiny.)* It got cold.
SIMEON:	Okay. *(Takes her cup, it's clearly still hot.)* I'll get you a fresh one, and then I have to go.
MARGARET:	*(Calling after SIMEON as he exits.)* And can I get another slice of hardo bread, toasted? Please? Thank you, sweetie.

> *MILLICENT enters. She has her own key. She is bottled sunshine, always smiling and positive. A personal support worker who lives in the building and a long-time friend of the family, she's begun taking care of MARGARET while she's on disability.*

MILLICENT:	Kumusta, everyone. Oh. It's so nice and cool in here. It's hotter than Manila in my place now.
RICHARD:	Morning, Milly. How you do?
MILLICENT:	Still living in God's glory.
MARGARET:	Amen.

> *SIMEON enters with a steaming cup of tea, handing it to MARGARET.*

MILLICENT:	Hello, Simeon.

He nods curtly at her.

RICHARD: You pray for me to win the lotto? Seventeen million big ones, you know.

MILLICENT: I pray for your safety and good health. If you get some money in the meantime, then you are doubly blessed.

MARGARET: Don't encourage him, girl.

MILLICENT: You ever win, Richard?

RICHARD: Do I look like someone who's ever won anything?

RACHEL: *(O/S.)* He won $20 a long time ago.

RICHARD: That was a good day! If I win that money, I'll have so much, *(Gleeful.)* I'll have to give it away! You'll be the first, Milly.

MARGARET: *(Gets puffed up.)* Excuse me?

RICHARD: Sorry, Milly, the second. But, wait now, Meggy. How many times I hear you complain that I spend too much money on lottery tickets, and now you asking, "What about me?"

MARGARET: I said no such thing.

RACHEL comes in with breakfast.

RACHEL: It's true, Daddy. I heard her. Morning, Millicent.

MILLICENT: Hey, Rachel.

MARGARET: Good sir, when you win the lottery, you're taking me on a cruise. One of them long ones, all over the Mediterranean.

MILLICENT: That sounds nice.

MARGARET: I hear Greece is real pretty and I've always wanted to try that fried cheese. How you fry cheese, anyway?

RACHEL: You wouldn't catch me anywhere near those floating deathtraps. After what happened to Grandma?

RICHARD: Deathtraps. It was a bad ting to happen fe true…

Everyone gets quiet and thoughtful.

SIMEON: Either she was pushed, or she fell.

MARGARET: Well, her balance was terrible, and the only person who would want to murder my mother was me.

Everyone looks at her.

What? *(Peevishly.)* She was my mother, I can say what I want.

MILLICENT: An accident like that should have gotten you some kind of payout.

She looks around for an answer. Collective silence.

RICHARD: She's fish food now.

MARGARET: I don't like to think about it. She never got a proper Jamaican send-off.

The sound of a dog barking repeatedly from a distance begins but nobody responds except RICHARD, who stops to listen intently.

RICHARD: How you grow up on an island and not know how to swim?

SIMEON: Swimming wouldn't have saved her. She could have been swimming and swimming and swimming, but if nobody saw her, she'd have gotten tired and—

MARGARET: Don't forget sharks.

MILLICENT: *(To RACHEL.)* I'm with you. Forget being trapped on a boat with a bunch of strangers and not being able to get off, seasickness, small cabins if you're not rich, rapes—

MARGARET: Rapes?!

MILLICENT: Oh yeah. I've read some horror stories about women who were attacked by crew members—

MARGARET: Ai! Stop, just stop now. I don't need no bad stories before noon.

MILLICENT: And, of course, there're the suicides.

                Everyone's eyes dart to look at SIMEON.

MARGARET: Milly!

MILLICENT: What?

SIMEON: I should brush my teeth.

                SIMEON exits.

RICHARD: *(Looks out the window.)* Man, these construction people waste no time. Can't wait to tear up our neighbourhood, eh? Not even 10 am yet.

MARGARET: *(To MILLICENT.)* Simeon's going to a funeral today.

MILLICENT: One of his army friends died?

                MARGARET nods.

MARGARET: Poor thing. She was a nice girl, too.

RICHARD: Back home, when someone die, you celebrate! You celebrate their life with whole heap a singing, dancing, and stories about them for the people left behind.

MILLICENT: Like a wake.

RACHEL: Better. Yeah, nine nights of celebrating the dead.

MARGARET: *(To RACHEL.)* How you know about dat?

RACHEL: *(Defensively.)* I know things.

MARGARET: And if you don't have that night, the duppy will get yuh. Boo!

MILLICENT: Ahhh, back home we call it multo; evil things that can take revenge on the living.

MARGARET: Same thing with us!

MILLICENT: You ever see a duppy?

                   RICHARD and MARGARET share a look.

RICHARD: But you should see the dancing! Hoowee! Meggy, we must show her. *(He starts flipping through vinyl albums for the right kind of music.)*

MARGARET: What? No.

RICHARD: Let's show them how it's done, my sweet girl.

MILLICENT: Oh, I like this.

RACHEL: *(Embarrassed.)* The dance is kinda, it's—

RICHARD: It's a likkle bit of dutty wining…

RACHEL: *(Mortified.)* Ahhh!

MARGARET: Look at this one. Such a prude.

> *RACHEL rises, taking the vinyl from her father, placing it on the turntable. She drops the needle and music fills the space.*

RICHARD: Come. *(Holds his hand out to MARGARET.)*

RACHEL: Millie, play this.

> *RACHEL passes MILLICENT a shekere, grabs the djembe and begins a percussive beat.*

RACHEL: Just shake it.

MILLICENT: *(Deliciously scandalized.)* Dirty dancing at a funeral? Sinful.

RICHARD: *(He speaks as he dances.)* First you have to get down and pat the ground like suh, make contact with the earth, the world. And, see you have to roll your leg like suh and move your hips like this, you see. And you must have a girl there like this young thing here. You want to entice her, remind her, that you have the goods, you know? And then you dance together, all smooth-like, right? Because we want to remind the powers that be that death will not conquer us. We can still mash it up. We are defying death and saying, "See me nuh? I am life!"

MILLICENT: This looks like a good way to send someone off to our Lord above.

MARGARET: You can talk 'bout our Lord above with this one shaking himself like that?

RICHARD: Hey, you're no church-girl right now, Mrs. Whyte!

MILLICENT: I don't feel like I'm in any danger. Now you? I'd watch it. Especially with that hip of yours.

MARGARET: Wooo!

MARGARET is slightly winded; she sits down and starts fanning herself vigorously with one of the number of fans strewn around the room. RACHEL stops drumming and takes the shekere from MILLICENT.

Now that's what I call a workout.

RICHARD: Think back to when we met and that was just, just the uh, uh, uh, appetizer. I knew you couldn't resist when I start wining. I tell you, when I would wine round me waist, the ladies couldn't stay away.

MILLICENT: Such a charmer!

RICHARD: And that's how you keep the duppy away!

MARGARET: *(To MILLICENT.)* See, I was looking for more of a Richard Roundtree—

RACHEL: Rest in peace—

MARGARET: —but I end up with this Dick instead.

MILLICENT: Don't think you can get out of going for our walk because of that little shake and shimmy. We need to get that heart rate up for more than a few minutes.

MARGARET: *(Whine.)* Do we have to go today? It's so hot!

MILLICENT: I have coconut water in my bag. You'll feel better once you're up.

RICHARD: Now don't wear her out too much, Milly. We have big Jamaican dinner planned.

MILLICENT: What's on the menu?

RICHARD: Rice and peas, oxtail with spinners, coleslaw—

MARGARET: That reminds me, don't forget to soak the rice.

RICHARD: I won't forget.

RACHEL: Margaret's cooking, not him.

RICHARD: Nobody makes fried dumpling like her. Ah lawd...cornmeal dumpling...dumpling dumpling...heaven! I try, but her hands are magic.

MILLICENT: You know what else is magic? Ordering in. It's too hot to cook. Give your wife a break.

RICHARD: She's the only one I trust to cook on this day.

RACHEL: Besides, most of the good Jamaican places are in the east end now.

RICHARD: You know I can't remember the last time I crossed the bridge to go there.

MILLICENT: *(To RACHEL.)* You can't get good fried fish and plantain around here because "the thing that shall not be named" killed any remaining businesses that were already having a hard time.

RICHARD: I miss Sunshine Bakery and their coco bread.

MILLICENT: This doesn't look like the neighbourhood I moved into over twenty-five years ago.

MARGARET: But change is good, sometimes.

MILLICENT: I moved here for a change. But too much change can be destructive. Imagine how my government could survive not one or two, but multiple coups? So many... Corazon did her best, but I hated seeing all those soldiers in the street, all the time, every single day. You know what soldiers are like when given their orders—

SIMEON enters the room slowly and he's in company dress, everyone stops to look at him.

SIMEON: No, please finish, Ms. Flores. You know what soldiers are like when given orders... what? What are we like?

Awkward pause as the temperature in the room seems to shift.

MILLICENT: I was talking about my history. Not about you.

MARGARET: Now don't get upset. We was just talkin'.

SIMEON stares at MILLICENT with... what? Hostility? A challenge of some kind?

MILLICENT: *(Rises.)* I just remembered that I left my water bottle upstairs. Meet you in front of the building in five minutes, Margaret?

RACHEL: *(Quietly.)* Wow, Sim.

He looks over at RACHEL.

MARGARET: Make it seven. I'm still cooling off and I have to drink my tea. Woo...it takes forever to cool down now *(Fans herself harder, but this time with a different fan.)*

RICHARD: And dinner is at seven, Mil.

MILLICENT: Oh. *(She looks at SIMEON quickly.)* I'm invited?

RICHARD: You part of the family, girl. Of course.

RACHEL: But think West Indian time.

MILLICENT: So, eight, then?

RACHEL: Ish?

MILLICENT:	What should I bring?
RICHARD:	I always like that chicken thing you make with the vinegar.
MILLICENT:	Chicken adobo coming up. *(To MARGARET.)* Don't forget to put on sunscreen.

MILLICENT exits.

MARGARET:	*(Yelling after her.)* Black people don't need sunscreen!
RACHEL:	Tell that to Bob Marley.
MARGARET:	Sunscreen is just another way for white people to take fools' money.
SIMEON:	*(To RICHARD.)* Can I borrow the car?
RICHARD:	As long as you put gas in it, the keys are by the door.
MARGARET:	That wasn't kind, Simeon!
SIMEON:	*(To MARGARET.)* What?
MARGARET:	You made Millie feel bad.
SIMEON:	I didn't make anyone feel anything.
RACHEL:	She was just telling a story and you were really rude to her.
SIMEON:	I don't like hearing people shit on soldiers.
RACHEL:	She was telling a story, you made it about you, and acted like a jerk.
MARGARET:	Rachel.
SIMEON:	Do you see how I'm dressed right now?
RACHEL:	Oh, here we go!

MARGARET: Rachel.

RACHEL: Any time someone tries to hold you accountable for the things you say or do, it always comes back to "I'm a soldier; you should respect me."

MARGARET: You should respect him.

RACHEL: For what?! His service was years ago. *(Starts to leave but turns back.)* Stop hiding behind your military service. We've all dealt with shit.

>   *RACHEL exits and walks into the kitchen where we see her try to relax her shoulders, gripping the counter and taking deep breaths. She eats some porridge from the pot, looks over her shoulder to make sure she's alone, removes a pill from her pocket, and takes it with water. She stares into the distance.*

MARGARET: Just ignore her. *(She stands and places her hands on SIMEON's shoulders.)* I'm proud of you, sweetie.

SIMEON: Thanks, Mummy.

MARGARET: See you later. Millie's waiting.

RICHARD: *(To SIMEON.)* Pick up some ginger beer on your way back.

MARGARET: And Richard, don't forget to soak the rice, you hear?

>   *MARGARET exits.*

RICHARD: I hear ya the first time, man!

SIMEON: It's either gas or ginger beer, I can't afford both. I'm strapped right now.

RICHARD: Okay. No problem. I'll get Rachel to pick some up.

                He thinks for a moment, pulls out his wallet, and hands SIMEON a ten, with a wink.

SIMEON: Thanks.

RICHARD: Where's the funeral?

SIMEON: Uhhh… *(Pulls a crumpled piece of paper from his jacket.)* MacGuire Funeral and Cremation Centre.

RICHARD: Mmhmm. Better get on the road, then.

SIMEON: Okay. Thanks for the car. *(He begins to exit.)*

RICHARD: She being buried or burned?

SIMEON: *(Halts.)* What?

RICHARD: They burying her or cremate?

SIMEON: I…don't know…

RICHARD: Okay. Just curious.

                SIMEON looks at him for a second and leaves. RICHARD peeks through the window onto the street.

I don't want them to burn me, you hear? Bury me. Bury me nice and deep.

                A dog on the street begins barking, and RICHARD's demeanour changes.

Go on…she not here. Bother someone else. Just stop, stop, you hear me.

Scene Two

Same. Moments later.

RACHEL walks in without RICHARD seeing her and she hears her father talking.

Rachel: Daddy?

RICHARD turns and looks at her, not surprised.

RICHARD: Hey, girl.

RACHEL: Who you talking to? *(Teasingly.)* Talking to yourself?

RICHARD: No. There's that dog, you know. The one that just sits down there and barks.

RACHEL walks to the window and looks down. Shakes her head and sits down.

RACHEL: I've never heard any dog.

RICHARD pulls out a small box from behind an armchair and begins removing small Jamaican and Canadian flags. He plants them all over the room throughout the scene, eventually popping one in RACHEL's hair.

RICHARD: We need to make this place look more Jamaican. *(Hums the Jamaican anthem tunelessly.)* You know who's Jamaican?

RACHEL: *(This is an old call and response that every immigrant kid knows.)* Who?

RICHARD: Rihanna!

RACHEL: No.

RICHARD: Yes. I see it on the internet. We should play some of her songs today.

RACHEL: What's the big deal about this year?

RICHARD: Forty years since I move to this country.

RACHEL: Ohhhh.

RICHARD: And it almost never happen.

RACHEL: I think you've told me this sto—

RICHARD: I was supposed to move to Chicago. But, see here: they nuh let me in. I get off my flight and them say, "No, go back." So, I get back pon de plane, fly back to Montego Bay, talk to some people and here I am. Toronto. And I love it. *(Closes his eyes and shakes his head with a smile.)* I love it so much, I don't even want to beburied back home. This is my country and I never regret not moving to America. I mean, look at that place now...you couldn't pay me. Get cigarette, they kill yuh, sleep in yuh car, dem shoot it up, pay by cheque and dem foot pon your neck. Bwoy...it so much better here.

RACHEL: Canada isn't perfect.

RICHARD: But it's better than down there. United States? *(Kisses his teeth.)* Just call them the States, because there's nothin' united about de place. If they hadn't sent me back, maybe I'd end up dead, or in jail, or in the nuthouse. Who can say... You should be happy I brought you here.

RACHEL:	So, you left Jamaica right after I was born?
RICHARD:	Shortly after…yeah…. I didn't plan that.
RACHEL:	Because I wasn't planned.
RICHARD:	*(Scoffs.)* Planned? That's a white thing. Babies just happen. You were a…surprise.

> *RACHEL takes this in as she removes books from the shelf and piles them on a living room table.*

Everybody like a surprise.

RACHEL:	I have a surprise for you.
RICHARD:	You won the lottery.
RACHEL:	Ha, I wish. It'll happen to you before it happens to me since you're the only one who plays.
RICHARD:	You can't win if you don't play! Eh, so these tickets you buy me… *(Pulling out the lottery tickets she gave him earlier.)* how you pick the numbers?
RACHEL:	Quick Pick, it's just faster.
RICHARD:	Ah….so that's why I never win anything. Rachel, you have to pick the numbers yourself. Shortcuts never win you nothing.
RACHEL:	Work harder at playing the lottery. Got it.
RICHARD:	Thank you fi buying the tickets the last couple of weeks. I promise to pay you back when I get my pension. Or when I win the lottery!
RACHEL:	Don't worry about it.
RICHARD:	*(Peers at her.)* You have a man now, Ray?

RACHEL: What? No! What would make you think that?

RICHARD: Ah, I don't know. You haven't been around much. When you *are* home, you stay in your room, and always run out of here if your phone ring. I figure, some big love affair.

RACHEL: Oh no, no boyfriend. No time to date. You see how much I work.

RICHARD: I do see, making the big bucks, helping out here. You doing well, girl. Really well.

RACHEL: *(Touched.)* Thank you, Daddy, I really appreciate you noticing.

RICHARD: Oh, I notice, I notice everything. Lemme ask you something.

RACHEL: Yeah?

RICHARD: *(Sweet and shy.)* Can I get a likkle loan?

RACHEL: How much?

RICHARD: Uh...two, three hundred.

RACHEL: Three hundred dollars? What for?

RICHARD: You know, if I went to a bank and ask for a loan, they wouldn't ask me what it's for, as long as I promise to pay them back.

RACHEL: That's not true and, you've never paid me back. Not once.

RICHARD: You work plenty job, makin' all this money, you nuh have no man, so you can help your father out, yeah?

                RACHEL stares at her father, considering him for a long time.

RICHARD: What?

RACHEL: I'm going to be making mortgage payments on my new place soon.

RICHARD: Mortgage?

RACHEL: I'm…moving out.

RICHARD stops what he's doing.

RICHARD: Why?

RACHEL: Because I should have my own place by now.

RICHARD: Should… *(Shakes his head.)* Who says? You'd rather pay rent in this expensive city than live with your family?

RACHEL: I won't be paying rent. It's a mortgage.

RICHARD: How you have money to buy a place?

RACHEL: I've saved. A lot. Everything I make. And you know I've always worked a lot of jobs, never go on vacation, don't buy new clothes.

RICHARD: Or lottery tickets…

RACHEL: *(Pause.)* Yeah. I've seen you and Margaret renting your whole lives and going with you on so many walks through model homes that you could never afford and wouldn't be buying…and I didn't want that kind of… future.

RICHARD: Nothing wrong with dreaming… Roommate?

RACHEL: No. Just me. I'm doing this by myself, and I'll never live with a man unless he's my husband.

RICHARD: You'll be lonely.

RACHEL: I'm lonely now.

This puzzles RICHARD.

RICHARD: How you lonely here with your brother, mother, and me?

RACHEL: *(Pivot.)* I'm moving in the spring.

RICHARD: So...you still able to, you know, help us out with the rent? I mean, after you leave?

RACHEL: *(Long pause.)* I—I—

RICHARD: Because with me not working and Meggy off on disability, it already really tight, you know, so...

RACHEL: I wish I could. All my money has been spent on the condo.

RICHARD: *(Brisk.)* It's alright...okay. We just have to cut back a bit, you know. Spend ten dollar pon lottery instead of twenty, Walmart is always hiring, maybe get Simeon to pay a likkle rent.

RACHEL: I'm sorry, he doesn't pay rent?

RICHARD: He used to throw us a couple bucks here and there but, with no job—

RACHEL: He hasn't worked in months. He was a security guard, like, a year ago?

RICHARD: You know it's hard to find work now, Rachel.

RACHEL: And yet I managed to have three jobs at the same time.

RICHARD: Yeah, you're a real Jamaican for true, girl.

RACHEL: No...no, no jokes, Daddy. Am I the only person in this house that's actually working?

RICHARD is momentarily speechless.

Oh my God. THAT is why I'm leaving.

RICHARD: We a family. You don't get a thank you fi doing what you supposed to do.

RACHEL: I'm not supposed to be supporting the entire family. A family where I'm barely an afterthought.

RICHARD: Afterthought? What does that mean?

RACHEL: You forgot my birthday!

RICHARD: I have never forget your birthday. It's July 6!

RACHEL: June!

RICHARD: What?

RACHEL: June 6!

RICHARD: *(Confused.)* But wait...

RACHEL: D-Day, remember? You always called it daughter day? But this year you forgot.

RICHARD: You know my father never remember my birthday? Never. Not once. With my mother, him have fourteen pickney; me the oldest. I never see him, because him run 'round town with all kind of ooman. Me have, like, fifteen...sixteen more brotha and sistas, me no know...Now, me? Me nevah look at another ooman as long as I've been married to your mother. She was it. She was the one.

RACHEL: She's not my mother. *My* mother, Claudia St. James, is still in Montego Bay.

RICHARD: Now you talk crap.

RACHEL: What's crap? That Margaret's not my mother or that you left my mom after she had me?

RICHARD: I sponsored you to come here. You wouldn't be here, with your fancy education, if you hadn't moved to Canada and had a much better life.

RACHEL: Who says my life wouldn't have been good in Jamaica? I would have been raised by someone who loved me.

RICHARD: How you know that? How you know she wouldn't have just pawn you off to her mother like plenty pickney in Jamaica?

RACHEL: —

RICHARD: You don't know, you don't. You see how hard it is to raise kids in this country as a single mother, but it never cross your mind what it's like in the islands. You know how many pickney raised by them grandparents? Plenty. At least here, you had me, Simeon, and Meggy. Full family under one roof. But you still not satisfied.

RACHEL: She never treated me like a daughter. I was a burden! Got in the way of raising her precious boy.

RICHARD: She raised you! What? You think you raise yourself? I wasn't around as much as I should have been but, ach, that was the time. Men work and women tek care of the pickney. That's it, okay? It wasn't like it is now with men walking 'round with baby strapped to them chest, walking a likkle dog like…like… I don't know what! Raising the kids was her job and she did it.

RACHEL: And I'm telling you that she raised one of us.

RICHARD: Look, when you were all likkle, she was the one who woke up before all of us, make us breakfast, make our lunches, fi me to take to work and you to school. She walked you both to school, help you with your homework, because she was the smart one between us. She made sure we had dinner every night. We nevah order pizza, or 'amburger, or any of that crap food because she took care of us. Before she do anything else, she put us first. You no see that? You no see that as raising her family? Raising you? Wha' you want, man?!

RACHEL: Love!

RICHARD: (Scoffs.) Love.

RACHEL: Why's that so ridiculous to you?

RICHARD: What we gave you was love. Maybe not the way you want it, but it was there.

RACHEL: Well, you did a shitty job.

RICHARD: (Stung.) That's not nice, Rachel.

RACHEL: Fuck being nice.

                     RICHARD is struck silent.

RICHARD: If I didn't want you, would I've brought you to Canada?

RACHEL: Caring for your kids shouldn't be optional.

RICHARD: (Exasperated.) I cared fi you! Why you say I don't care?

RACHEL: Because that's what it felt like.

RICHARD: I don't know what you want me to do about that now.

RACHEL: Paying for me to be here and putting a roof over my head isn't parenting.

RICHARD: Where we come from, it is.

RACHEL:	Doing the bare minimum wasn't enough. You never came to watch my choir performances, or that play in high school, or—
RICHARD:	I worked eight hours on my feet at the paint factory and all I wanted when I got home was a beer, dinner and sleep.
RACHEL:	I'd see all my white friends getting flowers and cards from their family who showed up, but nobody came to watch me. It's about showing up, Daddy… and baking me a cake on my birthday wasn't going to win you Father of the Year.
RICHARD:	You know, I have no idea if my daddy love me. None. Could have pass him on the street and not know him from a can of paint. But my mummy…I was her first child and she love me. Even when she beat me, I knew she love me.
RACHEL:	Doesn't sound like love to me…
RICHARD:	Wha you want me say?
RACHEL:	*(Pause.)* That you're sorry.
RICHARD:	Sorry!?
RACHEL:	Yeah. I want you to apologize.
RICHARD:	Fe wha?
RACHEL:	For not protecting me. For…not understanding how hard it was for me moving here from another country when I was a child.
RICHARD:	You were seven!
RACHEL:	Yes! A child.
RICHARD:	Ach! Nobody apologize to me when I get here.

RACHEL:	You were an adult! You chose to move to another country.
RICHARD:	I ain't apologizing for nothing. Whoever hear such thing. Parent apologize to pickney. *(Kisses his teeth.)*
RACHEL:	It happens all the time!
RICHARD:	Maybe with white people. That's the problem: You spend too much time around white people.
RACHEL:	Maybe if you hadn't—

MARGARET enters, breathless, sweaty, followed by MILLICENT.

MARGARET:	Lawd have mercy, it hot! It hot, it hot, it hot! Hoooo! *(Throws herself on the sofa and kicks off her shoes.)*
RACHEL:	You're back early.
MARGARET:	Thank you, merciful Father, for air conditioning.
MILLICENT:	We had to cut the walk short. It's so hot the air looks wavy.
MARGARET:	Richard? You soak the rice?

RICHARD looks caught.

I swear I have to do everything around here.

RICHARD:	*(Rises.)* Let me start on the rice and brown the oxtail.
MARGARET:	What you been doing since I gone? I see you've been decorating. Looks nice.
RICHARD:	If only we had some plastic palm trees, you know?

RICHARD exits to the kitchen where he dawdles and gets distracted as he measures the rice but forgets to soak it. He takes a big bowl, containing the marinating oxtail, from the fridge and places it on the counter. He pulls out a Dutch pot and starts chopping onions, garlic, and thyme.

MILLICENT: Let me go take a shower, start the chicken, and come back to help you relax your muscles. Drink some coconut water, Margaret. You don't want to get dehydrated.

MILLICENT exits.

MARGARET: You'd think we never have coconut water in Jamaica. Telling me to not get dehydrated…

RACHEL: She's just doing her job.

MARGARET: I'm nobody's job. *(Long pause.)* So, it feels like I interrupted a serious conversation between you and your father.

RACHEL: *(Shrugs.)* It's nothing.

MARGARET: *(Looking around the room and seeing the pile of books.)* What's going on over there? Reorganizing the living room?

RACHEL: *(Stands and crosses to pick up the books.)* Just packing up some things.

MARGARET: Oh? *(She's fanning herself lazily.)*

RACHEL: *(Long pause and then very direct.)* I'm moving out.

MARGARET: Good.

They stare at one another for a long second. RACHEL exits. MARGARET fans herself a little faster.

Scene Three

The same.

50 minutes later.

MARGARET is sitting in an armchair, her feet soaking in a basin of warm water and Dettol. MILLICENT slightly massages one of MARGARET's shoulders with Tiger Balm.

MARGARET: You know I never wanted kids? I wanted to finish college, become an interior decorator, and have a beautiful loft and now...

MILLICENT: And now you have two beautiful kids.

MARGARET: Rachel is my stepdaughter. She belongs to her father.

MILLICENT: I mean, I knew she wasn't *yours* yours...I just thought, since you raised her from the age of, what was it, eight, that she belongs to you, too. Upsie daisy now.

As MARGARET lifts her feet, MILLICENT slides the basin out of the way and replaces it with a towel. MARGARET sits up, leans over and begins drying her feet. MILLICENT walks to the kitchen to dump the water in the sink and returns.

MARGARET: People would say, "Oh you're so lucky, you have a boy and a girl." Lucky? Girls are hard!

MILLICENT: *(Dismissively.)* Bah!

MARGARET: I'm telling you, you don't know. Listen up, you get pregnant, pray for a boy. Boys are easier.

MILLICENT: All children are a blessing, auntie.

MARGARET: Yes, but *(Lowers voice.)* some are more of a blessing than others, that's all I'm saying.

MILLICENT: —

MARGARET: How old you now, Millie?

MILLICENT: Forty-eight.

MARGARET: Yeah? You keep good for forty-eight.

MILLICENT: I know.

MARGARET: I keep tellin' you. You pretty. Real pretty pretty. And you never wanted kids, eh?

MILLICENT: I'm an auntie many times over. That's enough for me.

MARGARET: And no man, eh? I gotta say, I envy you. Free to do what want, go wherever you like.

MILLICENT: Tell my bills that.

> *They're silent as MILLICENT stimulates the circulation in MARGARET's arm.*

MARGARET: Are you sure you're not…? *(She holds her wrist limply.)*

> *MILLICENT drops MARGARET's arm.*

MILLICENT: Mrs. Whyte!

MARGARET:	*(Mock shock.)* What?
MILLICENT:	You know what you did. Just stop it, okay?
MARGARET:	I wouldn't judge you if you were a fruit fly.

> *MILLICENT crosses her arms and glares at MARGARET sternly. MARGARET, avoiding eye contact, jumps up and walks to the bookshelf and pulls out* The Secret, *holding it up in triumph.*

I mean, they're everywhere. My old boss was one. Yes! And she was a pretty girl, too! Good hair, nice skin, a little fat fat, but nice face, you know? Maybe that's why she was funny. Into girls, I mean. *(Thoughtfully.)* But men like fat girls, so…I don't know.

MILLICENT:	You can't help who you fall in love with. I don't need to tell you that.
MARGARET:	What you mean by that?
MILLICENT:	Nothing. I—uh… nothing.

> *RICHARD enters. He's wearing a wide-brimmed straw hat and running shoes.*

RICHARD:	The rice is on, oxtail simmering. I just have to—
MARGARET:	Where you going?
RICHARD:	We need lima beans for the oxtail, and we outta ginger beer.
MARGARET:	Ask Rachel / to get it.
RICHARD:	/ *(Guilty.)* NO. Leave her.
MILLICENT:	I have some upstairs. You want me to get it?

RICHARD:	I already have me hat on. Besides, I need the walk and I haven't seen Mr. Chin in a long while. Check ya.

RICHARD exits.

MILLICENT:	Who's Mr. Chin?
MARGARET:	The man who run the small grocery store with the fruit outside and junk inside.
MILLICENT:	You mean Larry? Larry Kong?
MARGARET:	*(Shrug.)* We call him Mr. Chin.
MILLICENT:	And you don't think that's racist?
MARGARET:	Black people can't be racist! Besides, plenty Chinese in Jamaica and they all answer to Mr. Chin because Chin is a popular name there.

RACHEL enters.

MILLICENT:	I don't like it.
MARGARET:	You don't have to like it.
RACHEL:	Don't mind me, I'm just grabbing one of my books.

MARGARET hands her The Secret.

RACHEL:	That is definitely not mine.
MARGARET:	*(Quietly.)* Huh, maybe it is mine. *(Starts flipping through it.)*
MILLICENT:	Rachel, what do you think about calling Asian men "Mr. Chin"?
RACHEL:	I've already been called a bleeding-heart liberal who's too sensitive/ for saying it's racist so…

MARGARET: / Come now. Why do you even care? You're not even Chinese.

MILLICENT: The puti don't know that. When people yell "chopsticks and rice" or "ching chong" at me, it really hurts. Your words make me feel bad and this is the one place I don't want to feel that way.

MARGARET: *(Getting up and hugging her.)* Oh no, no, no…I don't ever want to hurt you, my likkle Millie. Don't you know you're like a daughter to me?

                      RACHEL reacts to this with a shake of her head.

                 I won't say Mr. Chin around you again. Promise.

RACHEL: I can't move out of this place fast enough.

MILLICENT: You're moving?

MARGARET: Got her own place. *(Begins fanning herself.)* Moving on up and out. *(She stands up and begins to exit.)*

MILLICENT: Where you going?

MARGARET: I'm going to go for a likkle lay down. I have a headache and my hip is still aching.

MILLICENT: There are stretches you can do for that. Do you want me to show you?

MARGARET: No, sweetie, I'm fine.

                      MARGARET exits and goes to the kitchen where she opens a bottle of pills and takes two with water. Pauses, looks behind her to make sure she's alone and takes one more pill.

> *RACHEL resumes pulling her books off the shelf as MILLICENT watches her for a bit. RACHEL looks over at her periodically and then stops.*

RACHEL: What?

MILLICENT: How are you doing? Really.

RACHEL: *(Shrug.)* I'm fine.

MILLICENT: No, you're not. What are you taking?

RACHEL: *(Lying.)* I'm not taking anything.

MILLICENT: My job is to take care of people, some are self-medicating. I see you chewing a lot of gum. That's for the dry-mouth, right? Dark circles under your eyes so your sleep is garbage. The tiredness makes you feel like you're dead on your feet, yeah?

RACHEL: I'm a zombie.

MILLICENT: You might need to take some melatonin.

RACHEL: *(Looks over her shoulder and lowers her voice.)* I'm on something for depression. Please keep that in the vault. Daddy and Margaret don't believe in drugs or therapy.

MILLICENT: You're a grown woman taking Celexa for depression, you don't have to be ashamed.

RACHEL: I can't afford Celexa, it's the generic stuff. I'm not ashamed, not really. It's just, if they knew, I'd never hear the end of it. I don't have the strength to deal with them making fun of me for needing to take medication. You should have heard them earlier talking about crazy people and suicide this morning because of Nadine—

MILLICENT: *(Alarmed.)* You're not having thoughts of—?

RACHEL: No. No, no, no, no, nothing like that. It's the sleepiness and general exhaustion that's really hard.

MILLICENT: Antidepressants aren't enough, though.

RACHEL: I might be taking a little... Adderall...just to give me some focus.

MILLICENT: Oh no, Rachel! I mean, I'm not your doctor, but that's not a good combination. Cut the Adderall and get a therapist. Zoom if you have to.

RACHEL: Zoom? In this apartment with a family that think personal space is a foreign concept?

MILLICENT: Okay. How about this? I'm going to give you a key to my place that you can use anytime you need half an hour or whatever, to talk to someone. Just give me notice and I'll book seeing a client at that time.

RACHEL: Why are you being so kind to me?

MILLICENT: I see a lot of my younger self in you.

RACHEL: How?

MILLICENT: I also have a *(Shoots a look in the direction of the hallway.)* difficult mother. It's one of the reasons I left the Philippines and never looked back.

        RACHEL sits.

RACHEL: I thought you moved here for a job.

MILLICENT: Sure, but, like you, I'm the oldest girl. And you know everyone looks to you to fix everything and ask for nothing in return. I was expected to accept less, but give the most, and I did.

RACHEL: Because if you didn't you were selfish.

MILLICENT: Exactly. If we had chicken for dinner, the boys got the meat while I had to make do with gravy and rice. If I made five dollars, my mother took four. It's to help the family, she said. So, I escaped. You're escaping, too, I get it.

RACHEL: I've had no life. Just work, work.

MILLICENT: It'll all be worth it when you're in your own place, not having to share a bathroom, nobody yelling, *(Imitation of MARGARET.)* "Rachel! Rachel, come nuh!"

RACHEL: *(Laughing.)* You do that really well.

MILLICENT: She reminds me of my Ina, a little. A terror in fuzzy slippers.

RACHEL: You know!

MILLICENT: Which condo did you buy?

RACHEL: They're called the Rhodium Towers.

MILLICENT: Oh yes, I've heard of them. Real fancy.

RACHEL: They're near the Bluffs so the view is so pretty.

MILLICENT: I put an ocean between me and my family. Crossing the bridge in this city is almost the same thing.

RACHEL: Moving out will be good for all of us.

MILLICENT: There's not a day that goes by I don't thank myself for choosing me first.

RACHEL: And you don't feel guilty?

MILLICENT: I used to. You'll get over it.

RACHEL: Pinkie swear?

                MILLICENT proffers her little finger and they "shake" on it and smile. MILLICENT and RACHEL's phones ding. MILLICENT stands.

MILLICENT: Time to check the chicken and see another client. See you at dinner?

RACHEL: Yup. Hey, how are you so... okay?

MILLICENT: Prayer.

RACHEL: *(Disappointed.)* Oh.

MILLICENT: And Zoloft, going on twelve years now. The Lord can't do everything.

RACHEL: Good talk, Millie. Thanks.

                MILLICENT exits. RACHEL pulls out her phone, scrolls and dials.

                Hi, may I speak to Daniel? Rachel Whyte. No, I don't mind holding. — Oh, hey, Dan, got your email, what's up? No, I didn't get any letter...

                We begin to see smoke coming from the kitchen, but RACHEL doesn't notice.

                I'm sorry, I don't understand. I signed a contract. — I get that but, what does that have to do with me? No, no, no, no, no, you don't understand how I feel. I don't know how I feel right now. *(Urgent.)* I'm — So, what am I supposed to do now? — Calm down? I, oh, shit! *(Looks at phone.)* My phone is dying. Daniel? Daniel??

RACHEL looks at the phone. It's dead. There's the sound of a loud crash from the street. The smoke detector comes on. MARGARET runs in from her nap, bleary eyed, wig askew, and disoriented.

MARGARET: Fire! We on fire! Rachel! Rachel!! Oh no oh no oh nooooo! Raaaachell?!

The home is filled with smoke; RACHEL is in a state of shock.

MARGARET runs into the kitchen, grabs the pot of burning food and dumps it into the sink, running cold water over it.

RICHARD comes in, carrying a case of Ting and whistling.

RICHARD: Crane across the street just crash down pon another building! Dust everywh— But what all this noise dis?

He rushes into the kitchen where he sees MARGARET dumping the second pot into the sink as well.

Ah no! Meggy, what happened? It all bun up? *(Kisses teeth.)*

MARGARET: Ask your daughter.

RICHARD: *(To RACHEL.)* Girl, wha'pen?!

MARGARET disables the smoke detector. They both exit the kitchen to the living room and look at RACHEL who has the thousand-yard stare, she doesn't acknowledge them. MARGARET opens the window and is shocked by what she sees.

MARGARET: Well, would you look at that.

The power goes out.

Mother of God, not now! This damn construction!

The land line rings and RICHARD answers jovially

RICHARD: Yo! Heeeey mannnn! How you do? — Happy Independence Day to you, too! — *(Laughs.)* Oh, you know, surviving! Still waiting for the big numbers to hit, you know! Meggy good, Rachel alright and Simeon out on the street now but we getting prepare to have big, big dinner. Callaloo and breadfruit? Maybe me should come to you, eh?

MARGARET has slumped onto a chair, fanning herself vigorously, RACHEL is a statue, RICHARD is smiling and nodding to the conversation as they're all enrobed in smoke. The dog starts barking.

RACHEL: It's gone…it's all gone.

End of Act One

ACT TWO

Scene One

> *Same. It's 7:30 pm. The smoke has cleared.
> The power still hasn't returned.*
>
> *Drooping tiny Jamaican flags punctuate
> the space. There's dust on everything from
> the construction outside.*
>
> *MARGARET enters, sits down, wipes her
> brow with a napkin and picks up a paper
> fan; fans vigorously.*
>
> *MILLICENT and SIMEON (now in
> civilian clothes) are in the kitchen. She's
> washing the dishes and he's drying. As she
> hands him a clean plate to dry, he takes her
> hand, holding it for a moment. She pulls
> it away.*

MILLICENT: No.

SIMEON: I said I was sorry.

MILLICENT: Could you…step away a little, give me some space?

> *SIMEON steps back and puts a plate in the
> cupboard.*

MILLICENT: In case I didn't say before, I'm sorry about Nadine.

MILLICENT: Did you see some of your old buddies?

                SIMEON nods and gets a faraway look in his eyes.

SIMEON: It was weird.

MILLICENT: Was there anything after?

SIMEON: A few of us went to a bar and had a couple drinks. *(Steps towards her.)*

MILLICENT: *(Definitive)* What did I tell you? We can't be together anymore.

SIMEON: Because...

MILLICENT: Because this is not real. Because I'm convenient for you. Because I live upstairs, you can see me whenever you want, and we never have to struggle to make plans.

SIMEON: Sounds perfect. What's the problem?

MILLICENT: I pay for everything. I plan all of the things we do, which isn't much because you won't leave the apartment.

SIMEON: If we lived together, I'd be different.

MILLICENT: Live together? No! And no, you wouldn't.

SIMEON: Fine, we can go out more. Where do you want to go?

MILLICENT: New York. Chicago, so I could see Wrigley Field.

SIMEON: You don't even like baseball—

MILLICENT: No, but my mom does. I want to take a selfie there and send it to her.

SIMEON: I didn't know that...about your mom.

MILLICENT: Well, you never asked.

                SIMEON leans against the counter with his head lowered.

SIMEON: Okay. I see.

MILLICENT: Do you?

                SIMEON is quiet for a moment.

SIMEON: No. I mean…no.

MILLICENT: What we had was fun and I loved being with you but—

SIMEON: You want more.

MILLICENT: Don't you? Is this really enough for you?

SIMEON: It's fine. For now.

MILLICENT: "For now" can turn into forever. I don't want that, and honestly, even though they drove me crazy, I miss my stupid, yelling family, I do. Your family made me realize that.

SIMEON: *(Rueful.)* My family?

MILLICENT: Do you see what's happening here? To your family? You have it so good.

SIMEON: Keep your voice down.

MILLICENT: You can't see it because you're dealing with so much shit.

SIMEON: You're going to tell me to go to therapy again, are you?

MILLICENT: You're a grown man who has to make his own decisions. And your lack of decision making about your life is holding me back. That's my fault because I thought I could fix you.

SIMEON:	I just need more time.
MILLICENT:	I don't have any more time.
SIMEON:	Okay. Okay, okay, okay. I just…I know you're right. But, what am I going to do now?
MILLICENT:	There you go again, asking me to fix you.

SIMEON is silent and sullen.

You need to be here, in this home, with your family. Your sister takes on way too much. Maybe you could, I dunno, shoulder the burden a little more. She's struggling.

SIMEON: You're so caring and considerate and…

Puts his hands around her waist and pulls her close, her arms hang straight at her sides.

…that's why I love you so much.

He leans in to kiss her, she weakens and just as she's about to give in, MARGARET enters, and they jump apart.

MARGARET: Eh, eh!!

MARGARET bolts from the room. SIMEON attempts to follow her, but MILLICENT holds him back.

MILLICENT: Let her be. Just give her space.

MILLICENT wipes her hands on a tea towel as SIMEON angrily takes a glass from the cupboard and a bottle of bourbon from a high shelf.

MILLICENT takes a gigantic trifle out of the fridge, grabs some paper dessert plates and walks it out to the living room.

> *SIMEON yanks the freezer door open and pulls out an ice tray that has RICHARD's wallet sitting on it. SIMEON is momentarily confused. MARGARET has poured herself a large drink.*

> *RICHARD enters the living room, rubbing his stomach. He looks out the window.*

RICHARD: Millie, you saved the day. And wha' dis? Trifle? Girl, you a mind reader. *(Serves himself a big spoonful.)* Ah wha you call that noodle ting you bring for dinner?

MILLICENT: Pancit.

RICHARD: And it was good, even though it wasn't hot. I like my food hot. But, it taste nice. Good with that chicken…a wha' it call? Adobe?

MILLICENT: Adobo.

RICHARD: Yes, man. Chicken adobo and noodle. I mean, it no oxtail and rice, cuz it bun up but you save us. You saved the day, Millie.

MILLICENT: It was nothing.

RICHARD: Now where is Rachel? She miss dinner, no call, nothing. I don't understand that girl sometimes.

MILLICENT: There's leftovers for when she comes home.

> *SIMEON enters, drink in hand, and sits down. MARGARET pointedly looks at him and then at MILLICENT.*

RICHARD: Now, you see. You're a good girl. A good daughter, I bet your parents miss you back home

> *RACHEL enters, looking exhausted and run-down.*

Hey, girl! We missed you.

RACHEL: What do you want from me now?

RICHARD: Eh?

RACHEL: *(Looking at MILLICENT.)* You should just adopt her, so you can have your perfect son and daughter.

SIMEON: Come on, now.

RACHEL: So much confidence as you hold that glass of rum I bought.

SIMEON: This is bourbon that I paid for. What's your problem tonight?

RACHEL: I really hate it here right now.

SIMEON: Yeah? Me too.

RICHARD: What de hell is happening right now?

RACHEL: You can't hate it here. You're the golden boy who can do no wrong. How could you ever hate it here?

SIMEON: Cuz I'm a fuck-up with no job, no direction.

RACHEL: Cheers to that!

MARGARET: I am so fed up with you, you hear me?

RICHARD: Margaret.

MARGARET: No. She's never happy. *(To RACHEL.)* Who do you think we are, eh? I'm no Michelle Obama and your father is definitely no Barack. You best stop expecting any of us to hold your hand and tell you everything's going to be okay. *(Kisses teeth.)*

MILLICENT: I should go. *(Starts to get up.)*

MARGARET: You stay right there.

> *MILLICENT shrinks down in her seat.*

You're soft, alla you pickney here. Nobody taught me how to be an adult. I just was. Nothing comes easy, all right? I moved to this country when I was a teenager and—

RACHEL: *(Tired, she's heard this before.)* I know. You made a life for yourself and—

MARGARET: Don't interrupt me when I am telling you something you don't know. And there is so much you do not know, Rachel. When I moved to Canada I had to live with a woman who just loved to beat me. Auntie Hyacinth… *(Quietly.)* She was the colour of weak tea and twice as bitter. She beat me, she beat me, lawd have mercy, she beat me. And it didn't matter what she could find. Slipper, spoon, belt, didn't matter. Said I was stuck up, and you know what, I was. I didn't care if that woman liked me. I knew I'd get out of there one day. My mother sent me here to have a better life. That was her showing me love. Auntie was a terrible woman, but I believe she loved me, even with a belt in her hand. And you should count yourself lucky that I never used a belt on you.

RACHEL: But you did hit me.

MARGARET: Once! *(To the group.)* And you know what she says to me when I picked up that slipper to give her just a little tap? She says, "I'm going to tell my teachers that you hit me." You see? She smart. Get me by crying child abuse.

RACHEL: Well, it worked, didn't it? You never hit me again.

MARGARET: Because your father told me not to.

RICHARD: Listen, Rayray, I didn't know how bad you were feeling back then, but, believe me, you were much better off here than in Jamaica.

RACHEL: The only thing that made me happy every year was getting a birthday card from my mom. She never missed my birthday, unlike some people. *(Glares at them.)*

             RICHARD and MARGARET exchange a look.

MARGARET: Oh yes, the birthday cards. You still have them?

RACHEL: Yes.

MARGARET: What else do you remember about those cards?

RACHEL: They always had money. Usually a crisp ten-dollar... *(Remembers, and confusion crosses her face.)* Wait...

MARGARET: A crisp what?

RACHEL: But...it was Canadian money. How is that...? I don't understand.

RICHARD: A lie to cover the truth.

MARGARET: For twenty-five years I've had to listen to you talk about your mother like she was Mother Teresa, and your daddy was perfect.

RACHEL: I never said he was perfect.

MARGARET: Well, you know how they say the truth will set you free? Let me tell you something.

SIMEON: Uh-oh...

MARGARET: Your mother never sent you a card on your birthday. Not once. It was me.

RACHEL: No, I remember the envelope, the stamp—

MARGARET: Faked. We always had plenty mail from Jamaica.

RICHARD: We just steam off the stamps and reuse them with some glue.

MARGARET: You could barely read when you move here, and we knew you didn't know what her handwriting looked like, so that part was easy.

RACHEL: I can't believe this.

MARGARET: It was your father's idea to put the money in the card. I said you'd catch on because the money was Canadian, but you never did.

MILLICENT: Wow.

SIMEON: That's some next-level deception.

RACHEL: How could I have been so stupid?

MARGARET: Children are stupid, and he's a tricky one, your father. He fooled me, too, long ago. I shouldn't have been surprised.

RICHARD: Fool you? What?!

MARGARET: Oh yes, sweet-talking Yardie at a party, and me, a nice girl. I was a nice girl from Hanover Parish, spoke good, speaky-spokey them call it, no patois, with a future and he stole that from me saying I couldn't get pregnant if we only had sex once. *(Points at RICHARD.)* Liar.

RICHARD: Me never lie to you. You talking crap now.

MARGARET: There I was, pregnant, no support from my mother, or anyone, so I married your father. And you know what day we marry, right?

MARGARET/

RICHARD: Halloween!

MARGARET: I really get a trick and a treat with this one.

RICHARD: I don't think that's fair.

MARGARET: I marry you and you get your papers. Isn't that right?

RICHARD: Lawd God, not this again!

MARGARET: I mean…he was smart—

RICHARD: Thank you—

MARGARET: —but he got lucky—

RICHARD: Lucky?!

MARGARET: —and because I loved him so much, I didn't turn him in to Immigration.

RICHARD: Listen to her, "turn me in," like I'm some kind of criminal—

MARGARET: But then he tells me, "Ohhh, but wait…I just remember, I have a daughter back home and I'm bringing her here." And Rachel, when you stepped off the plane, you look just like your mother.

RACHEL: You knew my mother?

MARGARET: Of course I did. Everybody knows everybody in Jamaica. You're pretty like her. No tree grown pon your face.

MILLICENT:	I'm starting to feel like I'm watching one of my teleserye.
RICHARD:	Your mother have a hard time back home. She call me and seh, "Dickie, you must tek her, I cyan't do this," and so I send fi you.
MARGARET:	Just because you want something, doesn't mean you're ready for all the responsibility that comes with it.
RACHEL:	I wish I didn't know any of this.
MARGARET:	She had no help to raise you.
RICHARD:	And it's not that she didn't want you, she just knew she couldn't give you what we could give you here.
RACHEL:	I really missed having a mother take care of me. I deserved that.
MARGARET:	Deserve... You learn that in therapy?
MILLICENT:	Therapy helps, Margaret.
MARGARET:	*(To MILLICENT.)* Are you a cuckoo bird, too? This...therapy. *(Scoffs.)* You chat, chat, chat about what? It nuh make you feel any better. Telling your problems to strangers?
SIMEON:	Well, it's not like we could talk to you or Daddy.
MARGARET:	About what? You're fine. We're fine.
SIMEON:	No, we're not, we're a mess!
RICHARD:	Who's "we"? I'm not a mess.
SIMEON:	Haven't you noticed that Mummy sleeps a lot?
RICHARD:	She tired.

SIMEON:

Taking so many pills? And Rachel is obviously unhappy, wait, no, depressed. I think she might be on pills, too.

RACHEL /
MARGARET:

I'm not *on* pills!

MILLICENT:

You shouldn't be talking about the medication they're on. Whatever they're dealing with, let them figure it out. At least they're dealing with their problems.

RICHARD:

Problems? What problems?

MARGARET:

Oh, didn't you know? These two are lovebirds.

RACHEL /
MARGARET:

What?!

MARGARET:

I caught them groping in the kitchen.

MILLICENT:

We broke / up

SIMEON:

/ It's complicated.

MARGARET:

Oh! Thank heavens. She's way too old for you.

MILLICENT:

I am not too old.

RACHEL:

Aren't you in your fifties?

MILLICENT:

I'm forty-eight.

RACHEL:

Mm.

RICHARD:

Simeon should be with someone he can start a family with and you're—

MILLICENT:

Old enough to serve you food, and take care of your wife, but not be with your son?

SIMEON:

(To himself.) I don't even know if I want kids.

RICHARD:	*(To Millicent.)* You are getting up there. More mutton than lamb.
RACHEL:	Daddy!
MARGARET:	It's like you've been lying to us all these years.
SIMEON:	Me?
MARGARET:	Her. *(Glaring at MILLICENT.)*
MILLICENT:	Me?
MARGARET:	Yes!
MILLICENT:	Why am I getting all the blame? He didn't tell you, either.
RACHEL:	Welcome to the family.
SIMEON:	Shut up, Rachel!
RACHEL:	Don't tell me to shut up.
SIMEON:	You've had a shitty attitude for a while now and you get away with it because you have ten jobs and help with the rent but, Jesus, it's exhausting to be around.
RACHEL:	Then move!
SIMEON:	—
RACHEL:	Yeah, exactly! You've floated through life free of all consequences. Now, you're here, living in this apartment where you *don't pay rent*. Your service ended years ago, and you still don't have a job. Everyone here is so easy on you, and it's always been that way.
SIMEON:	It never felt that way watching you get celebrated for going to university.

RACHEL: *(Scoffs.)* Celebrated. I did what was expected of me and I'm still paying off my student loans because you *(Pointing at her parents.)* didn't save any money for tuition.

SIMEON: *(Shrugs.)* Should have joined the armed forces and got a free ride.

RACHEL: *(Weighing the options.)* I dunno. PTSD or crippling interest? Tough choice.

SIMEON: How's that sociology degree workin' for you?

MARGARET: Nobody here told you to go to / university. That was all you.

RACHEL: / No no, but it was implied!

MARGARET: You could have gone to college, get a regular job without some fancy / title and—

RACHEL: / And what? Be like you and Daddy? Get laid off from your terrible factory jobs only to find yourself working at a grocery store?

MILLICENT: What's wrong with that?

MARGARET: Bitch, bitch. bitch, that's all you do.

RICHARD: Well, you're moving out, into your own condo, bought with your own money, which you couldn't have save if you nevah live here all this time. Remembah that.

RACHEL: *(Long pause.)* I lost the condo.

MARGARET: What do you mean you lost it? Just this morning you had it. How you lose it so fast?

RACHEL: The development company filed for bankruptcy. My $61,000 down payment... gone. I have nothing.

The power comes back on. The air conditioner is loud. Something crashes to the ground on the construction site across the street causing SIMEON to jump.

MARGARET fans herself slowly.

There's the faraway sound of a dog howling.

SIMEON pours himself a bigger drink. MILLICENT takes the mental health pamphlet and a card out of her bag and gives it to RACHEL.

RICHARD walks over to the window and peers out.

RICHARD: Oooowwwwooooo!

Scene Two

Audio and video reports of "urban renewal"—aka Black neighbourhoods being destroyed/eradicated for progress: Seneca Village (1857); Tulsa (1921); Rosewood (1923); Africville (1960s) Philadelphia (1985); Saint Antoine (1966); Hogan's Alley (1967); Little Jamaica (present).

Combined with similar stories of gentrification in other Canadian cities. Regent Park / Parkdale / Stanley Park, etc...

This pastiche of eviction and gentrification flashes in the dark, and begins to get smaller and smaller, until the theatre looks like as if it is filled with bright stars. Then darkness.

A tiny rectangular light illuminates a corner of the stage. It's RACHEL on her phone. Several hours have passed by.

RACHEL is overwhelmed with harsh fluorescent light. She's cross-legged on the floor of the hall closet, phone in hand, blinking up at RICHARD, who's just opened the door.

RICHARD: Is a hide you a hide?

RACHEL: Daddy.

RICHARD: *(Thrusts a phone receiver at her.)* Here.

RACHEL:	*(Takes it, covers the mouthpiece, and whispers.)* Who is it?
RICHARD:	It's Nancy.
RACHEL:	Who??
RICHARD:	Your Aunt Nan. Me sister, in Kingston.
RACHEL:	*(Incredulous.)* I haven't talked to her in ten years.
RICHARD:	*(Shrugs.)* She want to wish you a Happy Independence Day.

> *RACHEL looks at the receiver for a long moment, stands, and hands it back to her father.*

| RACHEL: | No. |
| RICHARD: | Rachel. Rachel come back 'ere! |

> *RACHEL walks out of the closet. She opens a cupboard to see too many six-packs of Ting! No ginger beer, though. She gets a glass from the cupboard, walks into the living room, pours herself some rum, and sits on the sofa.*

| RICHARD: | Rachel! *(He gets back on the phone.)* Hey, Nan. Dis gyal, you know how it is…I think she get into the Red Stripe…yeah. |

> *RACHEL enters with a bottle of Red Stripe and sits on the sofa. SIMEON walks into the living room and takes in his sister's mood. He pulls a photo album from the shelf and starts flipping through it.*

| RACHEL: | Let me drink my drink and be miserable. |
| SIMEON: | Funny. I thought I was the one who went to a funeral today. |

RACHEL realizes her insensitivity.

RACHEL: I'm an asshole.

SIMEON: A little. *(He sits beside her.)*

RACHEL: How was the service?

SIMEON: I…didn't go.

RACHEL: What do you mean you didn't go?

SIMEON: I couldn't do it. I started driving and I'm letting the GPS tell me where to go so I end up heading to the Viaduct and, of course there's the bridge to the Danforth and I can't do it. So, I turned onto Castle Frank Road and just drove.

RACHEL: I don't understand.

SIMEON: Bridges. Since getting back, I can't cross them. It takes me forever to get anywhere. Or I make an excuse not to go places. You don't realize how many there are until you have to cross another one.

RACHEL: Is this about what happened over there?

SIMEON: *(Lost in the memory.)* We were approaching a bridge, driving towards it, and I think we were just talking and laughing about something stupid, I'm sure. The vehicle ahead of us were from the French troops… good guys… and…I don't remember the IED going off. I can see the truck flying up in the…air and …there was a whooshing sound. Then glass, glass flying everywhere.

RACHEL: My god…

SIMEON: I could taste metal. Nadine was perfectly calm. I mean, the bridge was gone, a few bits hanging from the road, and the remains of the truck were in the water below. We were helpless. They were helpless, and we couldn't save them.

RACHEL: But you're not helpless anymore.

SIMEON: Gravity is certain, security isn't. I don't need to tell you that.

RACHEL: Sorry about the PTSD crack earlier. I'm really on a roll today.

> *A sober moment between siblings. RACHEL takes a drink and SIMEON begins flipping through the pages of the photo album.*

SIMEON: There's...not a lot of pictures of you in here.

RACHEL: Hm.

SIMEON: Most of them are—

RACHEL: —of you.

SIMEON: I was going to say, of me and you. Look at this one of us with Grandma.

> *They do not speak for a full minute.*

RACHEL: I miss her so much.

SIMEON: Why? She couldn't stand you.

RACHEL: What? No. She loved me. Loved me more than anyone here.

SIMEON: Other than me, of course.

RACHEL: Yeah, sure. But, seriously: she saved my life.

SIMEON: Come again?

RACHEL: When I was, I dunno, like ten, I was eating a piece of fried fish and, I remember, I was eating with my hands, like back home? But Margaret was like, use a fork, 'cause I think my hands were all covered in grease and onions. But when I used the fork, I missed one of those tiny bones, and started choking on it. Grandma saw me choking, put her hand down my throat, and pulled out the bone and that's why I only eat fish fillets.

SIMEON: Nope. You just bougie and don't like fish with the head.

RACHEL makes gagging noise.

SIMEON: Sorry, not bougie: Stoosh. That's what Grandma said about you.

RACHEL: Nuh uh. She was my hero.

SIMEON: Your hero was Mummy.

RACHEL: Hardly.

SIMEON: Grandma didn't save you that day, it was Mummy.

RACHEL: Nah, she would have let me choke to teach me a lesson about being more careful. She could be really mean to me.

SIMEON: I wish I knew. I would have protected you.

RACHEL: I was supposed to be protecting you, not the other way around.

SIMEON: Where is that picture? The one where you're in the plaid jumpsuit, maybe?

RACHEL: Ah yes, my Black Irish phase. Why didn't you tell me I looked like a lawn jockey?

SIMEON:	Would you really have taken fashion advice from an eleven-year-old?
RACHEL:	I begged Margaret to make it for me.
SIMEON:	And she said, "No."
RACHEL:	Repeatedly. Until...there it was in my closet when I got home from school.
SIMEON:	She kept saying no because she knew someone might snatch you up and put you on their front porch.
RACHEL:	I thought I looked so cute.

> *SIMEON jumps up and affects the pose from the photo: hand on hip, jutted out to the side, and a saucy pout.*

RACHEL:	You're so cute.
SIMEON:	And that's why I'm the favourite.
RACHEL:	Don't hold back now.
SIMEON:	I'm just repeating what was in your diary.
SIMEON/ RACHEL:	(*Gasp.*) How dare you?!
RACHEL	You read my diary?!
SIMEON:	You put it in the worst hiding spot ever.
RACHEL:	(*Pause.*) So...it wasn't Grandma who saved me. But I was her favourite!
SIMEON:	You weren't even in her will!
RACHEL:	None of us were.

> *SIMEON looks guilty.*

RACHEL:	(*Cautiously.*) How much did you get?

SIMEON: A grand.

RACHEL: Didn't she have a huge pension?

SIMEON: Yeah, and she went SKI'ing.

RACHEL: Huh?

SIMEON: SKI'ing: Spending Your Kids' Inheritance.

RACHEL: Ooooh. *(Pause.)* The church hats, nice shoes, the megachurch…the cruises.

SIMEON: Princess Cruises did very well by Mrs. Precious Reid.

RACHEL: I mean, good for her, I guess. How much did she leave Margaret?

SIMEON holds up his fingers in the shape of a zero.

RACHEL: NO! She got nothing??

MARGARET and RICHARD enter.

MARGARET: Oh yes. And it was just like you see on TV. Me and my sisters sitting there, finding out that not only has Mummy spent most of the money on herself, but we not getting a dime, and the Prayer Palace getting the rest.

RACHEL: But Simeon got a grand.

MARGARET: What?

RACHEL: The thousand dollars.

MARGARET: *(Softening.)* Ahh…

SIMEON: What does that mean?

RICHARD: Ignorance is bliss, Simeon.

MARGARET: Grandma didn't leave you a thing.

SIMEON: But what about the thousand dollars?

RICHARD: Your mother didn't want you to feel bad, so
               she picked up a couple of extra shifts at the
               store, and *(Shrugs.)* that's it. A lie to cover the
               truth. Nobody dies.

RACHEL: But why wouldn't she leave you anything in
               her will?

               *Dog howls. RICHARD looks toward the
               window.*

MARGARET: When I married your father, Mummy didn't
               approve.

RICHARD: She hated me.

MARGARET: She never think he was good enough for
               me. No college, rude bwoy, slick, him could
               dance—

RICHARD: Have you seen my moves?

RACHEL: Yes, Daddy. Earlier today.

MARGARET: —always a bad sign, and then he get me
               pregnant. I never forget what she say, "I
               didn't sponsor you so you could have some
               pickney out of wedlock."

RICHARD: And this from a woman who have four
               kids by three different man, suddenly clean
               because she born again? *(Kisses teeth.)* Duppy
               might get me fe dis, but me glad she die at sea.

MARGARET: She didn't have to be so mean to me. Children
               are supposed to be a blessing, right? *(Sigh.)*
               God may strike me down for dis but...I felt
               relief when she dead.

               *The howling stops—RICHARD's posture
               changes—freedom. MARGARET rubs his
               back.*

Come, sit.

They move to the sofa.

SIMEON: *(Huge sigh)* This family is a mess.

MARGARET: This family is normal! Everybody is miserable but doing their best. This ain't *The Fresh Prince* and I'm not Aunt Viv, no matter how much you want to replace me.

SIMEON: Nobody wants to replace you.

MARGARET: I never get to choose my mother and even though she was a cantankerous bitch, I miss her sometimes, but I manage.

SIMEON: You shouldn't have to manage, though. Because if you're just managing, how do you think we're doing?

RICHARD: You're adults. You manage. I mean, you have no job, but you have Millie, old as she is, and Rachel, you have your condo, job, and no man. But why need a man when you already have a place to live, amiright?

The family exchanges a look.

RACHEL: Daddy, I lost the condo.

SIMEON: And Millie and I broke up.

RICHARD: How?

SIMEON: Well, Millicent wants to travel and—

RACHEL: And the developer filed for bankruptcy.

RICHARD: *(To RACHEL.)* Bankruptcy? Since when?

RACHEL: Since today, when I told you. When I told all of you, a few hours ago.

Uncomfortable silence.

RICHARD: It's the first I'm hearing this.

MARGARET: Richard, she tell us, right after you almost bun the house down.

RICHARD: I'm old! I'm supposed to forget things.

                SIMEON hands RICHARD his wallet.

RICHARD: You turn pickpocket now?

SIMEON: And steal all your money? Never.

RICHARD: I ever tell you how I make the move to Toronto from Jamaica?

RACHEL: Yes. You're repeating yourself a lot tonight, Daddy.

RICHARD: I am?

                Nobody says anything, and RICHARD sobers. He sits quietly not making eye contact with anyone.

MARGARET: Eh, boy! You promised me you were going to be rich and take me on a cruise. Have you checked your lottery numbers yet today?

RICHARD: *(Brightening.)* Meggy! My queen. Let me go do that! We could be millionaires!

MARGARET: *(Tapping her lips.)* Come pay the tax.

                He leans down and gives her a short kiss.

RICHARD: Mmm, lips! Seventeen million smackaroos... oh lawd!

                RICHARD exits while humming; the room is still with silence.

                MARGARET turns to RACHEL.

MARGARET: It's better to be kind than right, sometimes.

RACHEL:	What? I couldn't listen to the same story again.
SIMEON:	I found Daddy's wallet in the freezer today.
RACHEL:	In the freezer? *(It dawns on her.)* Oh. Oh no. Does Daddy have—
MARGARET:	No, no, no…just let him be.
SIMEON:	How long have you been covering for him?
MARGARET:	I'm not covering for him! You're not here, neither of you. Just leave me alone. I don't want to talk about it!

MARGARET sits, heavily, defeated.

RACHEL and SIMEON find cases of Ting hidden everywhere. SIMEON sighs.

SIMEON:	*(Quietly.)* Shit shit shit shit shit…
RACHEL:	We're going to have to deal with this together.
SIMEON:	Do you think you can put in a good word for me at the warehouse where you worked?
RACHEL:	I can totally get you in, but it's a little far, if you know what I mean *(She gives him a look.)* It's in the east end.
MARGARET:	He can take the car!
SIMEON:	I'll take transit.

MILLICENT has entered quietly.

MILLICENT:	Did I hear you're getting a job?
MARGARET:	Hopefully.
RICHARD:	Hey, Million Dollah Millie!

MILLICENT: I'd like to think I'm worth more than that.

RICHARD: Sorry I call you fat earlier.

MILLICENT: You didn't call me fat, you called me old.

RICHARD: *(Shrugs.)* Eh, I'm old, too. Age mean wisdom. Same team, right?

MILLICENT: Team Richard, all the way. *(To RACHEL.)* You know, Rachel, I'm going to the Philippines in January for a visit. I'll be there for a few months, so you can stay in my place while I'm gone.

RACHEL: Interesting…

MILLICENT: I mean, it's no Rhodium Tower, but it'll be all yours. As long as you don't mind staying in the same building longer than you planned.

RACHEL looks over at MARGARET.

RACHEL: That's not a terrible idea.

RICHARD: Still thinking about that food you made tonight. So good. Tasty. Nice sauce. What you call it again? Adobe?

MILLICENT: Adobo.

RICHARD: Adobo…yeah, you must mek that again.

MILLICENT: It's a deal.

MARGARET: Please don't leave me, Millie.

MILLICENT: I'll find a good replacement, I promise.

RICHARD: You hungry, RayRay?

RACHEL: I'm fine.

SIMEON: I can hear your stomach growling from here.

RACHEL: *(Protesting weakly.)* I have this orange.

MARGARET: There's enough noodles for a few more meals.

                As MARGARET walks towards the kitchen she stops by RACHEL's chair, touches her hair, gently.

MARGARET: I like your hair like this. *(Begins to walk to the kitchen.)*

RACHEL: *(Surprised.)* Thanks....

MARGARET: You don't look like a boy anymore. Maybe now you can get a man.

                MARGARET exits and enters the kitchen where she takes the moment alone to let her shoulders drop and feel the end approaching. MILLICENT enters, putting a hand on her arm. She turns and in that moment there's forgiveness and understanding. They embrace.

RACHEL: I liked my short hair.

SIMEON: Just take it as a win.

RICHARD: I ever tell you I met the Queen?

RACHEL: No.

SIMEON: You did? Where?

RACHEL: When?

                MILLICENT re-enters and sits down beside SIMEON.

RICHARD: When I served in the Jamaican army. We fly to Britain, and I meet Queen Elizabeth.

MILLICENT: What was she like?

RICHARD: Very, very soft-spoken. And she smelled good, too.

SIMEON: I thought you hated the Monarchy.

RICHARD: Eh. *(Shrugs.)* she was nice, though.

MILLICENT: And that's how they get you.

RICHARD: She's still alive, right?

                Everyone exchanges a look.

RACHEL: Do you want to go back to Jamaica, get away from the Toronto winters?

RICHARD: No way. I already live in Little Jamaica, no need to go anywhere else...though I wouldn't mind visiting my mummy's grave...

SIMEON: Can we even call this neighbourhood Little Jamaica, anymore?

RICHARD: If all the Jamaicans leave, then, no, we can't. But, I'm not going anywhere, and neither is Margaret. When me dead, dig out the drywall, and seal me in.

RACHEL: I don't think that's legal, Daddy.

RICHARD: *(Laughs.)* Legal?! Just don't burn me.

                MARGARET enters with a small plate of food and hands it to RACHEL.

MARGARET: This conversation has gotten too dark.

RACHEL: Thank you...Mom.

                MARGARET really hears this, and she sits with RICHARD. The room is suddenly filled with the sound of rain.

MARGARET: Ah yes! Dutty tough no more!

MARGARET stands and opens another window.

RICHARD: *(Quoting.)* Rain a fall but dutty tough.

MARGARET: Nowadays the times are hard when/Yuh ask smaddy how they do—

RICHARD: —Dem 'fraid yuh tell dem back,/So dem nuh answer you.

MARGARET: No care omuch we da work fa/Hard-time still een wi shut;

Everyone turns to look at RACHEL.

RACHEL: We dah fight,/Hard-time a beat we/Dem might raise wi wages, but/

MARGARET: One poun gawn awn pon we pay, an/We no feel no merriment—

ALL THREE: For ten poun gawn pon wi food/An ten pound pon we rent![1]

MARGARET: Girl! You know your Miss Lou!

RICHARD: Of course she does, she's my daughter! Now, let's have a song.

RICHARD jumps up and starts flipping through some of his vinyl. He forgets what he's doing. Looks a bit lost until MILLICENT joins him and they look together until the rum catches his eye. He grabs it and a bunch of glasses with MILLICENT's help. RACHEL's phone dings three times, she crosses to her purse on the floor on the other side of the room, and pulls it out, dislodging a piece of paper that falls to the floor.

---

[1]   *From "Dutty Tough" by Louise Bennett Coverley. Reprinted by permission of Louise Bennett Coverley Estate.*

RICHARD: And let me pour us some Wray and Nephew. We not dead yet, right, girl?

MARGARET: Right, Dickie.

> *RICHARD pours everyone a shot of rum and hands them out. MILLICENT looks at RACHEL.*

MILLICENT: *(Whispers.)* Good news?

RACHEL: I may get some of my deposit back, but not for a while.

MILLICENT: I'm so sorry.

RACHEL: I can always make more money. I don't have many nights like this with my family left, right?

> *They both look at RICHARD. MILLICENT squeezes her shoulder.*

MILLICENT: Don't worry. I'll be back to help.

SIMEON: This fell out of your purse. *(Hands her a lottery ticket.)* Good luck.

RACHEL: Can't get any worse than today.

> *She looks down at the crumpled lottery ticket, shrugs and scrolls through her phone.*

RICHARD: You know what I want to really hear? Millie, what's the national anthem for your country?

MILLICENT: *(Singing.)* O Canada, our—

RICHARD: Stop ya foolishness!

MILLICENT: *(Laughing.)* Canada is my country!

MARGARET:	You have such a pretty voice, Millie. Sing for us, please?
MILLIE:	Okay, okay…
RICHARD:	But first, a toast. Stand up, everyone. Rachel, put down your phone. You have plenty time to look at it when ya in your new condo.
RACHEL:	Daddy, I— (*Stops at a sharp look from MARGARET.*) Yes, yes, you're right. (*She lowers her phone, but keeps sneaking peeks at it, brow furrowed.*)
RICHARD:	(*Clears throat.*) Bredren, Yardies, queens, and soldiers: Sometimes you got to take a likkle bit of sufferin' to get that hope. Happy Emancipation Day!
SIMEON:	Cheers!
	Everyone drinks.
RICHARD:	Millie, take it away!
	As MILLICENT begins to sing "Lupang Hinirang" in Tagalog, RICHARD gets distracted and looks out the window, face unreadable.
	The lights come down until we can only see RACHEL in a spotlight.
	MILLICENT gets more passionate in her singing. The lights start narrowing to a spotlight on RACHEL's face.
	MILLICENT's song ends.
SFX:	"Winner: Gagnant!"
	Blackout.
	The end.

Study Guide

The following study guide for Get That Hope *was created for the première production of the play at the Stratford Festival in 2024 and is reprinted by permission of the Stratford Festival.*

GRADE RECOMMENDATION

Grade 8+

CONTENT ADVISORY

The play explores mature issues including mental health, trauma, racism and colonization. Specific content warnings re: mentions of suicide and coarse language.

SYNOPSIS

Richard Whyte is determined to celebrate Jamaican Independence Day in style. The rice is soaking, the ginger beer is cooling and today his lottery ticket is finally going to hit it big! But Richard's squabbling family has other ideas. Over the course of a single sweltering day in Toronto's Little Jamaica, a lifetime of buried secrets and dreams will surface, forcing a re-examination of true independence.

CURRICULUM CONNECTIONS:

Global Competencies

- Citizenship, Collaboration, Communication, Creativity, Critical Thinking, Metacognition, Self-Awareness

Grade 8

∞ The Arts

∞ Health and Physical Education

∞ Language

∞ Science and Technology

∞ Social Studies, History and Geography

Grades 9–12

∞ The Arts (Dance, Drama, Music, Visual Arts)

∞ Canadian and World Studies

∞ English

∞ Health and Physical Education

∞ Technological Education

Grades 11–12

- Social Sciences and Humanities

Post-Secondary

- Suitable for courses in disciplines such as African-Caribbean Studies, Arts, Black Diaspora Studies, Canadian Studies, Caribbean Studies, Cultural Studies, Creative Writing, Drama, English, Fine Arts, Gender Studies, History, Human Rights, Social Development Studies, Teacher Education and Theatre

THEMES

- Aging and Memory
- Caregiving
- Colonization
- Duty, Familial Responsibilities and Expectations

- Filipino Culture

- Generational Relationships and Rifts

- Gentrification

- Jamaican Culture, Food and Tradition

- Home, Family and Belonging

- Hope and Despair

- Loss, Sickness and Death

- Mental Health

- Racism, Bias, Discrimination and Stereotyping

- Social and Economic Im/mobility

- Trauma, Truth and Memory

- War and Post-Traumatic Stress Disorder (PTSD)

DISCUSSION AND REFLECTION QUESTIONS

∞   *Get That Hope* by Andrea Scott focuses on the intergenerational conflict between members of a Jamaican-Canadian family; it is in part inspired by Eugene O'Neill's *Long Day's Journey Into Night*. *Get That Hope* explores issues of racism, colonization, gentrification, mental health and belonging. Why do you think playwrights write stories of family conflict to examine larger social issues?

∞   What do you know about gentrification? Have you witnessed any examples of it? If so, what impacts have you noticed?

∞   What is the relationship between suffering and hope? Can there be hope without pain?

∞ There is a tension in the play between the older generation's expectations around familial duty and the younger generation's hopes for their future. Why do you think these intergenerational conflicts are so prevalent, and how might they be resolved?

Several lines on page 102 are excerpted from the poem "Dutty Tough" by Louise Bennett Coverley. The following is a biography of "Miss Lou," who was an important figure in her native Jamaica and in her adopted home, Toronto.

Right Honourable Dr. Louise Simone Bennett Coverley OM, OJ, MBE

Louise Bennett Coverley was a Jamaican poet and activist. Born in Kingston, Jamaica on September 7, 1919, Louise Bennett received her education from Ebenezer and Calabar Elementary Schools, St. Simon's College, Excelsior College, and Friends College (Highgate). Her first dialect poem was written when she was fourteen years old. A British Council Scholarship took her to the Royal Academy of Dramatic Art, where she studied in the late 1940s.

On her return to Jamaica, "Miss Lou," as she became known, taught drama to youth and adult groups for both social welfare agencies and the University of the West Indies, but she soon became known for her poetry. Through her poems in Jamaican patois, Bennett Coverley raised the dialect of the Jamaican folk to an art level; she was able to capture the spontaneity of the expression of Jamaicans' joys and sorrows, their ready, poignant, (and even wicked) wit, their religion and their philosophy of life.

Miss Lou lectured extensively in the United States and the United Kingdom on Jamaican folklore and music and represented Jamaica all over the world. She married Eric Winston Coverley in 1954; together they raised her stepson and several adopted children.

Miss Lou's contribution to Jamaican cultural life was such that she was honoured with the M.B.E., the Norman Manley Award for Excellence (in the field of Arts), the Order of Jamaica (1974), the Institute of Jamaica's Musgrave Silver and Gold Medals for distinguished eminence in the field of Arts and Culture, and an Honorary Degree of Doctor of Letters from the University of the West Indies.

Louise and Eric moved to Toronto in 1987, where she quickly became an integral part of the community. She was awarded an Honorary Degree of Arts and Letters from Toronto's York University and was nominated for an ACTRA award for best original song for "You're Going Home Now" from the film *Milk and Honey*. Miss Lou died in 2006, and the following year on the anniversary of her death, "Miss Lou's Room," a reading room for children, opened at Toronto's Harbourfront Centre.

Louise Bennett Coverley's work continues to be read and studied, and her name is still a household word in Jamaica, Canada, and beyond.